"Dave Mulder's book is timely for today's educational landscape. He illustrates the worries and wonders of artificial intelligence, giving Christian educators bite-sized (or should I say 'byte-sized') concepts and cases to ponder. Instead of fear and hype about AI, he offers practical and wise insights through the lens of faith."

—**Rebecca Alburn**
Assistant Professor of Education, Corban University

"*Teach Like a Human* by Dr. David Mulder is a timely, refreshing guide for Christian educators navigating AI with wisdom and heart. He asks the right questions and offers practical applications for teaching and learning, all framed through a biblical lens. The bite-sized chapters are great for discussion and action. This is a must read for the Christian educator!"

—**Jared Pyles**
Instructional Designer, Cedarville University

"Dr. Dave takes the most pressing topic in education (and the world?) today and brings it down to Earth with a casual, practical, and human-centric approach. Whether you are just beginning to wonder about AI or are already comfortable using it, this book equips all educators with a healthy, nuanced, and Christian framework for understanding AI's impact in the classroom and in everyday life."

—**Joseph Jasper**
Educational Technologist, Capistrano Valley Christian Schools

"For anyone wondering if AI will ruin or revolutionize education, this book is for you. *Teach Like a Human* is the roadmap for AI integration which every Christian educator needs—a reminder of our place within the Big Story and vision for why decisions about AI in the classroom matter. With the wisdom and energy of Neil Postman, Dr. Mulder has adeptly balanced candor with humor, worldview with practice, and warnings with hope."

—**Jacob A. Hall**
Assistant Dean for Assessment and Accreditation, SUNY Cortland

Teach Like a Human

Teach Like a Human

Playful Practice and Serious Faith in the Age of AI

DAVID J. MULDER

WIPF & STOCK · Eugene, Oregon

TEACH LIKE A HUMAN
Playful Practice and Serious Faith in the Age of AI

Copyright © 2025 David J. Mulder. All rights reserved. Except for brief quotations in critical publications or reviews, no part of this book may be reproduced in any manner without prior written permission from the publisher. Write: Permissions, Wipf and Stock Publishers, 199 W. 8th Ave., Suite 3, Eugene, OR 97401.

Wipf & Stock
An Imprint of Wipf and Stock Publishers
199 W. 8th Ave., Suite 3
Eugene, OR 97401

www.wipfandstock.com

PAPERBACK ISBN: 979-8-3852-5841-3
HARDCOVER ISBN: 979-8-3852-5842-0
EBOOK ISBN: 979-8-3852-5843-7

VERSION NUMBER 091825

Unless otherwise indicated, all Scripture quotations are taken from the Holy Bible, New International Version®, NIV®. Copyright © 1973, 1978, 1984, 2011 by Biblica, Inc.™ Used by permission of Zondervan. All rights reserved worldwide. www.zondervan.com The "NIV" and "New International Version" are trademarks registered in the United States Patent and Trademark Office by Biblica, Inc.™

Scripture quotations marked (ESV) are from The ESV Bible (The Holy Bible, English Standard Version®), © 2001 by Crossway, a publishing ministry of Good News Publishers. Used by permission. All rights reserved.

To Missy,
love of my life,
my constant cheerleader
who loves me as my most-human self.

Contents

Acknowledgements | xi
Introduction | xv

Part I: The (Latest) Brave New World
  1 Artificial Intelligence: Problem? Panacea? Something Else Entirely? | 3

Part II: Stories, Imagination, and Technology
  2 An Imagination for AI: R2-D2, HAL 9000, the Terminator, and More | 9
  3 Examining Your Imagination: Stories We Tell Ourselves | 12
  4 Imagining Humans and Machines: You Are Not a Computer | 16
  5 Contours of a Christian Imagination: Seeing the Big Story of the Bible | 21

Part III: The Big Story and Why It Matters
  6 The Metanarrative of Scripture: Finding Our Place in God's Story | 27
  7 Creation: God Doesn't Make Junk | 32
  8 Fall: Everything Is Actually Awful | 36
  9 Redemption: Jesus Loves You! | 39
  10 Restoration: How Then Shall We Live? | 43
  11 Becoming a Truth-Seeker: Navigating Competing Stories | 47

Part IV: Demystifying Artificial Intelligence

12 Thoughts on Intelligence: Should We Be Worried About "Actual Stupidity"? | 53

13 Understanding AI—How Do Computers Work? | 57

14 Neural Networks: More Powerful Processing | 61

15 Machine Learning and Probability: Basic Ideas for Programming AI | 65

16 Large Language Models: Generating Responses to Your Prompts | 69

17 Garbage In, Garbage Out: Learning to Talk to a Computer | 73

Part V: AI and the Work of Teaching and Learning

18 Becoming, Not Arriving: Committing to Playful Practice | 81

19 Teaching and Learning: Two Different Could the "(but Related)" get moved up to the previous line?(but Related) Activities | 85

20 Rosie the Robot: Ensuring Humans Do the Right Work | 89

21 Doing the Right Work: Wisdom from Grandpa Mulder | 93

22 Ethical Implementation: Where the Christian Imagination Rubber Hits the Road | 97

23 AI and Discipleship: Avoiding an Educational Technology Arms Race | 102

24 Being Brave: Learning from Orville Wright | 107

Part VI: AI Use Cases

25 AI Use Case: Leveled Reading | 113

26 AI Use Case: Generating Review Questions and Scripts | 117

27 AI Use Case: Rubric Development | 122

28 AI Use Case: Creating Graphics | 127

29 AI Use Case: Personalized Tutoring Systems | 132

30 AI Use Case: Iterative Writing | 137

Part VII: A Theology of Educational Technology

31 Toward a Theology of Educational Technology: Living Faith in a Technology-Rich World | 145

32 Education as Formation: More Than Information Transfer | 149

33 The Role of Doubt: Cultivating a Humble Skepticism | 154

34 The Arc of the Redemptive Story: From the Garden to the City | 159

Part VIII: Launching into the Future

35 Christian Education and AI: Where Are We Headed? | 165

Bibliography | 169

Acknowledgements

WRITING IS IMAGINATIVE WORK, and there are many people to thank, each of whom helped this book move out of my imagination and into your hands.

Thanks to my friend Dr. Lynn Swaner for reaching out and encouraging me to write a chapter for ACSI's *Leading Insights: Artificial Intelligence*. Developing that chapter helped me clarify and more clearly articulate the bones of what would eventually become this book. Who knew when we met at a Christian education conference back in 2018, that a book about artificial intelligence would eventually result? The Lord truly works in mysterious ways! I'm grateful for your friendship and encouragement.

Another word of gratitude to Lynn, as well as to my new pal Paul Matthews (thanks for your excellent thought-leadership about teaching with AI, Paul!) for co-presenting a pre-conference workshop about AI for Christian educators at Converge 2025. It was a pleasure to collaborate with you both in that session, friends, and this helped me further refine the ideas in this book.

I would be remiss to not mention Edward Bunn, Director of Professional Development at ACSI, who was instrumental in helping me get this book from the dreaming stage into the writing stage. I'm grateful, brother!

I must recognize the brilliant AI Task Group I serve alongside at Dordt University. This is a wonderfully interdisciplinary group working on how we can navigate the opportunities and challenges of AI in a non-anxious, humanity-affirming, God-glorifying way

Acknowledgements

at our institution. My conversations with Dr. Tim Klein, Dr. Nick Breems, Dr. Brette Feldhacker, and Dr. Josh Matthews have helped me think both theologically and practically about what educators need when it comes to artificial intelligence and the impact it is having on teaching and learning.

Thanks to my friend Dr. Jared Pyles, who is a brother in Christ and fellow EdTech geek. Our conversations over the past year have helped me to develop and refine my thinking about ethical implementation of generative AI.

A huge "thank you!" to a couple of friends and colleagues at Dordt University who read early drafts of a few chapters of this book and gave their kind, specific, and helpful feedback. Dr. Gayle Doornbos, Associate Professor of Theology, provided helpful comments on the chapters laying out the metanarrative of Scripture, and I deeply appreciate her wisdom as a theologian and biblical scholar. Dr. Kari Sandouka, Professor of Computer Science, graciously allowed me to audit her Introduction to Python course several years ago, brushing up my programming chops. She also gave me valuable feedback on the chapters that address the hard technology aspects of AI—machine learning, large language models, and the like. I am so grateful for the encouragement from these dear colleagues, and the resulting work is stronger for their input. Any errors are mine, not theirs. I appreciate you so much, friends, and it's a pleasure to serve alongside you.

Speaking of friends, the Tuesday morning coffee crew at the Fruited Plain Café is always an encouraging bunch, and I love sharing life and laughter with you all. My fellow Dordtlings, you are an incredibly important part of my flourishing (heart, soul, mind, and strength), and I'm so grateful for you all. While I'm at it, I'd be remiss to not give a shoutout to the baristas at The Fruited Plain, who always make an excellent cup. They provide me the space and caffeinated beverages to do some of my best thinking: about two-thirds of this book was written there, fueled by their light-roast drip coffee and iced mochas.

Acknowledgements

Thank you to the Kielstra Center for Research and Grants at Dordt University for supporting the writing and publication of this book.

My deep gratitude to the wonderful team at Wipf & Stock for moving this project forward in such a timely way. You folks are a blessing.

The soundtrack for writing this book was provided by the lovely musicianship of Hollow Coves, The Oh Hellos, The Welcome Wagon, and The Paper Kites. I recommend all these artists for your listening pleasure.

Introduction

THE SEED OF THIS book began in 2021. I have the pleasure to facilitate a master's level course every other summer that is ambitiously entitled "Emerging Technologies." I find that I must continually redevelop the course every time I teach it, because of the joyful challenge of keeping up with the constant development of new educational technologies. That said, the general contours remain similar: one part looking at lessons from the history of educational technology, one part trying to imagine the hazy future that is just out of reach, and one part seeking to navigate the present as we find intended and unintended consequences of innovation. Our goal through it all: learning to develop schema for working with novel technologies in God-glorifying, humanity-affirming ways.

When I taught the course in the summer of 2021, generative AI was still lurking just over the horizon. Students had many questions, and I did as well! As you can probably imagine, by the time I taught the course again in the summer of 2023, our conversation was wildly different, as ChatGPT had burst upon the scene. Now, as I'm writing this book in 2025 and preparing to teach the course again, it's crazy to think how quickly things have shifted regarding generative AI, with a wide variety of different AI-powered tools at our fingertips. It's a little overwhelming, isn't it? But we have a real opportunity to learn, and to lead, and to keep discerning. I hope this book will be part of the conversation for Christian educators grappling with the challenging issues that emerging technologies bring.

Introduction

I am grateful to that group of insightful graduate students in 2021 for asking the thoughtful, thought-provoking questions that prompted me to start pondering, and researching, and writing a sort of theological approach to how Christians in education might address the burgeoning challenges and opportunities that generative AI would bring. It's a brave new world! But it's also good to remember that there is nothing in all of creation that is outside of Christ's sovereign rule and reign, thanks be to God! This truth gives me confidence as I continue to explore and as I continue to develop my thinking about the role of AI in my own teaching practice and professional life.

My deep hope is that this book will be a blessing for all Christian educators as they explore and consider the right role of AI in their professional work. I hope it will both challenge and encourage readers. And I hope it will provide a way of exploring the contours of a Christian imagination for both the possibilities and potential pitfalls of generative artificial intelligence in the teaching-and-learning endeavor.

Blessings to you all on the adventure!

Dr. Dave Mulder
Dordt University
June 2025

PART I

The (Latest) Brave New World

1

Artificial Intelligence
Problem? Panacea? Something Else Entirely?

IN THE FALL OF 1995, I had a life-changing experience.

I was a sophomore in college who had recently changed my major from computer science to elementary education. I received an email from my friend Jon, who was studying engineering at the University of Michigan. The email began, "Hey Dave . . . check out my website!"

I immediately wrote him an email back: "Hi Jon . . . what's a website?"

Now I realized that some of you reading this can probably *hardly imagine* that someone would have that response. I bet it sort of sounds like "What is this newfangled 'electricity' you're talking about?" or "Just what do you mean by 'indoor plumbing?'" Yes, you're right . . . I'm a Bona Fide Old Dude.™

But this was the reality: in the mid-1990s, the World Wide Web was brand-new, and it was still quite a novelty. While I was well-familiar with email and had dabbled with online bulletin board services, I truly wasn't quite sure what Jon meant by a "website."

Part I: The (Latest) Brave New World

He wrote me back with some instructions for the kind of computer I was going to need to find on campus, one with a piece of software called Mosaic, which was a "web browser." And then there was that weird string of characters he told me I would need to enter into a field at the top of the web browser window: "http://www.umich.edu/engineering/students/~Jon . . ." and so on.

I headed over to the computer center on campus and asked around about a computer that had Mosaic, and I soon found myself clicking on an icon for the web browser and slavishly typing in that string of one hundred or so characters that started with "http" and hitting Enter.

Slowly, slowly, slowly . . . one line at a time . . . a picture of my friend Jon in a characteristic tie-dyed T-shirt, rocking out with his guitar loaded onto my screen.

And I remember thinking to myself: "This. Will. Change. The. World."

Fast-forward a few years to the early 2000s. I had graduated from college and was a few years into my career as a middle school math and science teacher at a Christian school. I was regularly using the Web for my own work as a teacher. Google was introduced in 2001, which was a game changer. And I was beginning to imagine ways I might have my students use the Web as part of their own learning. We had a computer lab with twenty-five iMac computers that I could sign out for projects, and by 2003 I was regularly bringing students into the lab to do research online.

But it was also about this time that we started having a conversation amongst our faculty, asking, "What are we going to do about this World Wide Web thing?" Some teachers thought we should embrace it, as it was surely going to transform education as we know it. Others thought we should ban it outright. Still others seemed so overwhelmed that they just wanted to ignore it—asking the question, "Just how worried should I be about this?" We lurched along, and while some avoided the new technology, and some wholeheartedly embraced it, most ended up somewhere in between and learned to adapt their teaching and their students'

Artificial Intelligence

learning to incorporate the World Wide Web to at least some degree.

And here is the point of my story: the contemporary situation around artificial intelligence in education reminds me very much of my early adventures with the Internet. In fact, I suspect if you would replace "artificial intelligence" for "World Wide Web" in my initial story, you've probably had a similar sort of experience. Maybe you've had that sort of "what is AI?" feeling, not unlike my "what is a website?" question. Maybe thirty-some years down the line you are going be sharing your own story: "I remember the first time I entered a prompt into the text box for that AI chatbot and saw the output being generated and thought, 'This. Will. Change. The. World.'"

Because the truth is, the conversations I'm having with Christian educators today about artificial intelligence strongly echo those discussions from the early 2000s about the World Wide Web. Some folks view AI as something that is going to change the world and thus, we should enthusiastically embrace it. Other educators are intent on banning AI from schools, due to the problematic aspects. Still others seem overwhelmed by the prospects of what a world with AI means, in education in particular, and are asking that honest, heartfelt question: "Just how worried should I be about AI?"

Perhaps you can find yourself in one of those responses to artificial intelligence?

My deep hope is that this book will equip educators with an imagination for a what artificial intelligence is, and more than that, a *Christian* imagination for AI in education. I do not believe that AI is a panacea that is going to cure every ill for Christian educators. Neither do I view AI as an enemy to be defeated. I think artificial intelligence is a tool—a powerful tool, to be sure!—and one that educators need to approach with care and with wisdom. And in that regard, I hope that the Christ-centered approach in this book will encourage a thoughtful response to both the potential as well as the pitfalls of AI in Christian education.

So, let's wade into that messy middle ground, where we aren't going to single-mindedly champion AI, but neither are we going to seek to ban it. We certainly aren't going to bury our heads in the sand! Instead, we're going to explore a biblical perspective on what it means to be human, because AI seems to have some real implications for how we view our students—and ourselves. We're going to try to understand what AI is and how it works. We're going to investigate some examples of what AI might look like in practice in education today. And we're going to try to begin to develop a thoughtful theology of technology and innovation in education.

Artificial intelligence exists, and we are all going to have to adapt to this reality: it's a brave new world out there. But praise God that while things in this world may change, his word stands as truth forever and ever. Let's commit to lean on him, even as we keep learning and growing!

KEY IDEA FROM THIS CHAPTER

New technologies continue to develop, and human beings often must adapt in response to the cultural shifts that new technologies bring.

QUESTIONS FOR REFLECTION AND DISCUSSION

1. Do you have a "my first experience with AI" story? What was the setting? What did you do, and what did you learn?
2. Can you locate yourself in one of the responses to AI described in this chapter? Complete this sentence: "The idea of AI in education makes me feel ____, because . . ."

PART II

Stories, Imagination, and Technology

2

An Imagination for AI

R2-D2, HAL 9000, THE TERMINATOR, AND MORE

I HAVE A CONFESSION to make: I absolutely *love* science fiction stories. Stories of space travel, aliens, flying cars, and robots captured my imagination from childhood, and I still enjoy these kinds of books, films, and TV shows. You may or may not enjoy science fiction, but even if this is not your go-to genre for entertainment, I suspect there have been some influences on your imagination from sci-fi pop culture. Film and TV franchises like *Star Trek*, *Star Wars*, *Doctor Who*, and the Marvel Cinematic Universe have had a huge cultural impact, even for folks who might not gravitate towards science fiction.

Robots in particular have become an important part of our shared imagination—machines often created in replication of human likeness, or at least humanoid forms, or a kind of human-ish artificial intelligence. There is a long, long history in film of robots replicating human intelligence. From Robby the Robot in *Forbidden Planet*; to Rosie, the robotic maid on *The Jetsons*; to the droids in *Star Wars*; to Data, the android science officer in *Star Trek: The Next Generation*, there were many depictions of artificially

Part II: Stories, Imagination, and Technology

intelligent machines throughout the science fiction stories of the 1960s, '70s, and '80s. Many of these robots were illustrating positive representations of ways artificially created intelligences could help humans or providing interesting points of view for the stories being told.

But there is one exceptional example from that time period of an artificial intelligence that was definitely the antagonist of the story: HAL 9000 in *2001: A Space Odyssey* (1969). This is a clear commentary on the potential of an artificial intelligence to run amok and act in opposition to human characters. HAL introduced the trope of the artificially intelligent antagonist, created out of human hubris and providing the conflict the human protagonists must overcome.

From the 1980s to the 2010s, there were countless movies that used this evil machine trope to great effect. Picture Arnold Schwarzenegger as *The Terminator*, flatly warning human characters, "I'll be back." Or maybe Hugo Weaving as Agent Smith in *The Matrix*, coldly pursuing Neo and his friends inside the digital world. Or James Spader's terrifyingly sardonic Ultron in *The Avengers: Age of Ultron*, who believes he is on a righteous crusade? From *Tron* to *Blade Runner*, to *Robocop*, to *I, Robot*, to *Wall-E*, to *Ex Machina*... the list of malevolent artificial intelligences marches on.

All these examples might feed into our imaginations of what artificial intelligence is and how it might help or harm humanity. R2-D2 and Wall-E give us illustrations of helpful, cute, spunky robots who can save the day. The Terminator and Agent Smith suggest examples of the potential for existential threats to humanity. Ultron challenges us to wonder about the role human pride plays in the creation of artificial intelligences that might in fact destroy us. Characters like Data from *Star Trek* prompt us to ask questions like "What does it mean to be human?" and "Could machines have emotions?"

My point in all of this is not to advocate that you should watch any of these films or TV shows. Rather, I'm suggesting that you probably already have an imagination for artificial intelligence that is at least partially shaped by popular culture, and I want to

An Imagination for AI

call your attention to this. If we are going to understand our reactions to AI's influence in our world today, we better understand where our current thinking comes from. My argument is that you already have some kind of imagination about AI, and it didn't poof into existence out of nowhere. The media is a powerful influence on our imagination. And if we are going to respond wisely to the rapid technological changes that AI is bringing, we need to understand our own thinking.

More than that, I think we might need a better imagination for what AI is and how we ought to respond! What kinds of stories are you telling yourself about AI and your relationship to it?

KEY IDEA FROM THIS CHAPTER

Popular culture is a powerful influence on our imaginations for what AI is and how we should respond to technological changes.

QUESTIONS FOR REFLECTION AND DISCUSSION

1. Do you generally imagine AI as a good thing? A bad thing? A neutral thing?
2. What stories, films, TV shows, and other pop culture influences have shaped your imagination for what technology is and how humans can and should interact with technology?

3

Examining Your Imagination
Stories We Tell Ourselves

THINK ABOUT YOUR FAVORITE stories. What makes you love them?

Great stories have compelling characters, fascinating settings, and intriguing plot elements. But they also demand a powerful conflict, which is what drives the story forward. The hero must have a compelling adversary or a trial to overcome to make for a captivating story. Without a truly challenging conflict, there isn't much of a story to care about, is there?

You might be familiar with the idea of the "hero's journey," as made famous by Joseph Campbell in his book *The Hero with a Thousand Faces*. In this book, Campbell uses mythological stories across cultures to describe the journey taken by a hero in many stories. The hero's journey can be basically described in three steps:

1. The Call: The hero—who is often not very heroic at the outset of the story—is drawn out of their ordinary world and thrust into a bigger, wilder world where the adventure begins. The hero is guided into this new world by a mentor.

2. The Challenge: The hero, navigating the new world, is faced by a series of obstacles and meets both friends and adversaries

Examining Your Imagination

along the path. Eventually, the hero must face a great challenge which reveals their heroic nature.

3. The Return: The hero, having navigated the great ordeal, returns home to their ordinary life, but is changed by what they have experienced. They have a newfound power, or knowledge, or wisdom that they carry with them, fundamentally different than they were when they left.[1]

Does this story sound familiar to you? Maybe you're picturing Bilbo Baggins in Tolkien's *The Lord of the Rings* saga, or Luke Skywalker in *Star Wars*, or Katniss Everdeen in *The Hunger Games*, or Dorothy in *The Wizard of Oz*? Maybe Harry Potter, or King Arthur, or Lightning McQueen in *Cars*? *The Odyssey*, *Back to the Future*, *The Lion King*, *Moana* . . . at the core, all of these are stories that illustrate the hero's journey.

Perhaps my favorite example of a hero's journey is the story of Eustace Scrubb from C. S. Lewis's *Chronicles of Narnia*. Introduced at the beginning of *The Voyage of the Dawn Treader*, Eustace is . . . just *the worst*. Through the telling of the story, we find Eustace utterly transformed from a self-centered brat into an actual dragon, and then—after an encounter with the great lion, Aslan—back into a boy but now a tender-hearted and caring human who truly is a hero throughout the rest of the series. Lewis's work is a remarkable allegory of the Christian life, and perhaps the reason I best love Eustace's transformation is because it reminds me of my own need for transformation. It's a masterfully told story!

Humans are captivated by stories. We love tales of good and evil; we see the dramatic tension of different kinds of conflict, and we love to see our heroes succeed in the face of their struggles. Stories spring from our imaginations . . . and they also inform our imaginations.

We often talk about "imagination" as if it's "just pretend" or something kids do when they are playing. But I think that imagination is bigger and richer than *just* kids' stuff—though it certainly is something kids do too. It's a sad thing that many adults seem to have lost touch with the idea of imagination as a key part of our

---

1. Campbell, *Hero with a Thousand Faces*.

Part II: Stories, Imagination, and Technology

intellectual lives, because I think we all do have an imagination at work.

For example, you already have some picture in your head of what "artificial intelligence" is, and how it works. This is part of your imagination, and it is almost certainly shaped by the media you've consumed up to this point in your life. There is a sort of story that you are telling about AI, and this story is created out of your imagination. And I want to be clear about this: there's nothing wrong with telling stories! Humans are story-formed people, after all—we are always looking for ways to make sense of the world around us, and stories are a powerful way to not only get at the cognitive aspects of describing the world but also the emotional aspects of how we feel about the story we find ourselves in.

The story you are telling yourself about artificial intelligence might cast AI as the hero, or perhaps a mentor, or a loveable sidekick, or a henchman of the forces of evil, or perhaps the despicable villain itself. And where do you locate yourself in this story? Because you probably play a role in the story you're telling as well. Perhaps you're the hero? Maybe a henchman of the villain? Or a victim of the villain?

Have you ever thought about this story before—and what it reveals about your imagination?

Christian philosopher James K. A. Smith has a good bit about the role of imagination and the unexamined stories we tell ourselves. Smith says,

> To be human is to be on a quest. To live is to be embarked on a kind of unconscious journey toward a destination of your dreams . . . It is less an ideal that we have ideas about and more a vision of 'the good life' that we desire. It is a picture of flourishing that we *imagine* in a visceral, often unarticulated way—a vague yet attractive sense of where we think true happiness is found.[2]

Smith's point? We all have an imagination, and it sometimes (often) goes unexamined. We are part of a story, a story we are

---

2. Smith, *You Are What You Love*, 10–11.

Examining Your Imagination

telling about ourselves that help us make sense of our lives. The stories we tell ourselves are illustrations of what we deeply love, deeply fear, deeply desire.

Perhaps, like Eustace Scrubb, we are in need of a transformation of our imaginations—and the stories we are telling ourselves. We need to learn to tell better stories about who we are, the world we live in, and who is really in charge of it all.

KEY IDEA FROM THIS CHAPTER

We all have stories we tell ourselves, and examining these stories can help us better understand what we love, what we fear, and what we desire.

QUESTIONS FOR REFLECTION AND DISCUSSION

1. How do you picture yourself in the story you are telling yourself about artificial intelligence? Are you a hero? A villain? A victim?

2. What do you make of Smith's idea that our imaginations often go unexamined? What might that mean for the story you are telling yourself?

4

Imagining Humans and Machines
You Are Not a Computer

LET'S GET SPECIFIC ABOUT the work of our imaginations and the way we imagine computers in particular. How do you picture what a computer is and what it does?

That might seem like a silly question to ask, but in all seriousness, do you picture computers as *thinking machines*? There is an interesting thought experiment proposed by an early computer scientist named Alan Turing way back in 1950 that has taken on his name.[1] The "Turing Test," as it has come to be described, is a way of thinking about whether machines have a sort of intelligence that cannot be distinguished from human intelligence.

Here's the way the Turing Test works: a human judge is communicating with both a human and a computer, and if the judge cannot determine who is the real human, the machine passes the test for "intelligence." The machine is programmed to give human-like responses to the judge's queries, and the goal is for the computer to make the human judge believe it is also a human being.

1. Turing, "Computing Machinery and Intelligence." Turing called this thought experiment "the Imitation Game," which is also the title of a film about his life and the work he did to develop code-breaking computers during World War II.

Imagining Humans and Machines

The human judge is physically separated from both the human and the machine, and the judge can only give and receive text-based communication. Can you picture it? A person sitting at a computer terminal, chatting with both another human being and a machine, but communicating only by typing into a text box on the computer screen, and receiving text-based responses.

Now, this was a thought experiment, but I wonder if this scenario tugs at your imagination when it comes to the way AI chatbots work. Have you ever wondered if there is another human being on the other end of your computer connection when you type something into that text box?

Social scientist Sherry Turkle has been researching this sort of phenomenon for decades. Turkle is a professor at MIT and investigates human-machine interactions. In her book *Alone Together: Why We Expect More from Technology and Less from Each Other*, she shares the results of two streams of her research.[2] First, she describes how humans interact with robots and how regularly people assign human attributes and motivations to the machines—indicating a sort of imagination that people have for the robots. People in her studies describe the robots as having desires, thoughts, and even emotions, which is intriguing. The second stream of her research is equally troubling but in the opposite direction: she also researched social media's influence on human beings and how "virtual" connections cause us to talk about human relationships in more instrumental terms. In fact, Turkle's research indicates that the mediated interactions between people have tended to make us treat people more like objects. These two research streams are fascinating—and troubling—when taken together. There is a weird sort of leveling out between people and machines: humans begin to treat machines (objects) as more human-like while simultaneously treating human beings as more object-like.

Now, you might say, "I would never do that thought!"

---

2. I first read Turkle's work over a decade ago, and it has profoundly impacted the way I think about the role of technology in my own life, and the way I try to talk about machines. This book is readable, and while it's a bit "dated" now, Turkle's basic premise absolutely holds up and seems to be even more true today than when it was published.

Part II: Stories, Imagination, and Technology

Not so fast, friends. I encourage a little introspection for the way you use language. Do you ever describe the central processing unit of a computer as its "brain"? Do you ever describe human thinking as "processing"? Do you say "please" and "thank you" to the machines in your life? Do you ever apologize to the machines in your life? Do you ever catch yourself saying things (to real people) through digital communication that you would not say face-to-face?

I confess, when I'm honest about this, I sometimes do all these things. I treat the machines in more human-like ways, and I treat humans in more object-like ways. And I'm not proud of this—in fact, I don't like it at all!

The main reason I don't like this tendency in myself is because of what I actually believe about what it means to be a human being. My favorite depiction of what it means to be human comes from Andy Crouch's wonderful book *The Life We're Looking For: Reclaiming Relationship in a Technological World*. Crouch uses Jesus' own teaching in the Gospel of Mark, when a teacher of the law asked Jesus which commandment is the greatest, and Jesus' reply gives us an insight of what it truly means to be human:

> "The most important one," answered Jesus, "is this: 'Hear, O Israel: The Lord our God, the Lord is one. Love the Lord your God with all your heart and with all your soul and with all your mind and with all your strength.' The second is this: 'Love your neighbor as yourself.' There is no commandment greater than these."[3]

Crouch uses this passage as the basis of his beautiful depiction of what it means to be human: "Every human person is a heart-soul-mind-strength complex designed for love."[4] Doesn't that just capture the reality of humanity? You are not a body without a soul. You are not a mind without a body. You are not a soul without a heart. You are not a heart without a mind. You were never meant to be a soul without a body. And none of this matters without love!

---

3. Mark 12:29–31.
4. Crouch, *Life We're Looking For*, 33.

Imagining Humans and Machines

Later in the book, Crouch argues that so much of the appeal of technology is that it magically gives us superpowers. But the problem is that the superpowers for technology generally empower *one* of these dimensions of what it means to be human (heart-soul-mind-strength complex designed for love), and just like with superheroes, with great power comes a great weakness, an Achilles heel. For example, perhaps a technology can boost the powers of my mind, but this superpower comes at a cost, perhaps of my heart or my capacity to love my fellow human beings?

Perhaps this is why Sherry Turkle's findings are so compelling and so troubling: the superpowers that technology brings cause us to diminish our view of the humanity in the other people around us.

Crouch also encourages us to keep in mind that there is a difference between "something" and "someone."[5] We need to be careful of treating machines like humans. We need to be careful of treating humans like machines.

Humans are *not* machines. Machines are *not* human. The "intelligence" of a machine is *not* the same as human intelligence. The words we use matter, and they illustrate the reality of our imaginations!

KEY IDEA FROM THIS CHAPTER

Technology can have a strange influence on the way we view our fellow human beings, and as we live out our imaginations we might find ourselves treating computers more like humans and people more like machines.

---

5. Crouch says, "You do not have to become a person. You do not have to prove you are a person. As long as you have been and as long as you will be, you are a person. . . . [But] at certain places and times, we have sensed, even if we could not quite explain why, that we were being treated as *something* rather than *someone*" (p. 29). This difference between "something" and "someone" is a powerful way to picture what it means to be human!

Part II: Stories, Imagination, and Technology

QUESTIONS FOR REFLECTION AND DISCUSSION

1. Think about the way you use language about humans and machines. Can you think of examples of how you describe machines in human terms or humans in machine terms?

2. What do you make of Andy Crouch's definition of what it means to be a human being? Does this resonate with you? Does it help inform your imagination about the difference between humans and machines?

5

Contours of a Christian Imagination
Seeing the Big Story of the Bible

THINK ABOUT HOW YOU talk about the Bible. Is it a book of instructions for how to live? Is it an ancient collection of morality tales about what happens when people obey or disobey? Is it a compilation of different writings from different time periods? Is it an explanation of how things came to be? Is it an explanation of where things are going? Is it an introduction to the Christian faith?

What *is* the Bible? And what is the Bible really *for*?

I think that the way an individual describes the Bible illustrates some sense of their imagination—and particularly a *Christian* imagination. The way we see the Bible, and the way we describe what the Bible is, illustrates the way the Bible informs the way we think and even the way we act. This is to say, I think it really matters how we talk about Scripture!

We often talk about the Bible as being a book, and modern Bibles certainly are that: large books, all bound together. But it might be more accurate to describe the Bible as a *collection* of different books, written by different people (though all inspired by the Holy Spirit!) in different places, at different times in history, with different audiences, and different purposes for the writing.

Part II: Stories, Imagination, and Technology

The books of the Bible are in different genres as well. Some are history, like Joshua, 1 and 2 Kings, and Acts. Some are poetry, like Psalms, Ecclesiastes, and Song of Songs. Some are prophetic works, like Isaiah, Daniel, and Habakkuk. Some are letters, like Romans, Philippians, and James. And there are some books of the Bible that include multiple genres of writing; the book of Jeremiah, for example, includes some history, some poetry, some prophecy, and some letters, all collected in one lengthy book. And there are some special parts of the Bible unlike any other kinds of writing, such as the Gospels—Matthew, Mark, Luke, and John—which specifically tell us who Jesus is, what he did, and why it matters.

With all these various pieces of writing combined into one book, it's enough to perhaps make us wonder whether the Bible holds together at all! And so, it is perhaps not a surprise that different people have very different views of what the Bible is and what it is for. With the variety of different kinds of writing and different functions of the different parts of Scripture, maybe it really does make sense to think of the Bible as a kind of divinely inspired library?

But the Bible *is* one book, and the good news is that it *does* tell one story.

The Bible tells us the story of God and his people.

The Bible tells us . . .

- of a God who creates and sustains all things and has created people in his own image.

- of the way the people he created turned their back on him in sin, breaking relationships and tarnishing the goodness of what God has made.

- of a God who loves the people he made so much that he would go to any lengths to save them and heal the brokenness in this world.

- of a Restoration that is coming and is already in process through the actions of an all-powerful God and will fully appear when Jesus returns in glory!

This is the big story of Scripture: Creation. Fall. Redemption. Restoration.

This big story is the point of the whole book! God created. Humans ran away. Jesus came to save the day. God is making all things new. Woven throughout the sixty-six books that make up the Bible, we can see this one big story. And this big story shapes our imagination. Or, at least, it *should*. In the next section of the book we'll further unpack this big story to better understand how it can give shape to a distinctively Christian imagination, which we can use to explore AI.

KEY IDEA FROM THIS CHAPTER

The Bible tells one big story in four acts: Creation, Fall, Redemption, and Restoration, and the big story of Scripture shapes our imagination.

QUESTIONS FOR REFLECTION AND DISCUSSION

1. How do you describe the Bible? Or maybe, what do you think the Bible is *for*?
2. Can you think of various stories from the Bible that illustrate the four acts of the big story?

PART III

The Big Story and Why It Matters

6

The Metanarrative of Scripture
Finding Our Place in God's Story

IMAGINE THE BIG STORY of the Bible as a play being staged. It might be pictured as four acts:

- Act I is *Creation*. In this act, we see God at work, creating all things, making everything "very good," and laying out the norms for how things work in his world.
- Act II is the *Fall*. In this act, we see human beings rebelling against God, and we understand all the ways that things fall apart because of this rebellion.
- Act III is *Redemption*. In this act, we see that God has not turned his back on sinful humanity and goes to all lengths to save them—and redeem the whole Creation in the process.
- Act IV is *Restoration*. In this act we see God ultimately renewing all things, and in the meantime, we have foretastes of this ultimate Restoration, seeing God at work in the world and inviting human beings to participate in this Restoration in small, human ways.

Part III: The Big Story and Why It Matters

Understanding the big story helps us truly understand the little stories of Scripture. Theologians would call the big story the "metanarrative" of Scripture: the story that runs through the other stories and holds them all together. Now, while it's true that we can see these movements overall when we consider the Bible as a whole, the truth is a bit more complex and nuanced. It's not just the meta-story of Scripture that helps us understand the individual stories more fully: the themes or motifs of Creation-Fall-Redemption-Restoration can be found throughout the individual stories in Scripture as well.

Let's look at a few examples to illustrate what I mean.

Reading Gen 1 and 2, we see God's work of *Creation* very explicitly. But we can also see this throughout Scripture, from the poetic depictions of God's creativity and care in Ps 24:1–2, Ps 139, and Job 38–41, to stories of ongoing creating work, such as Elisha and the widow's oil in 2 Kgs 4, or Jesus feeding the five thousand in Matt 14. Romans 1:20 reminds us, "For since the creation of the world God's invisible qualities—his eternal power and divine nature—have been clearly seen, being understood from what has been made, so that people are without excuse." God creates, God provides, God sustains. Examples of his goodness—and the goodness of all the things he has made—are prevalent throughout Scripture!

Reading Gen 3, we see the *Fall* laid out explicitly as Adam and Eve disobey God and eat the fruit they were told not to eat. But we can also see the brokenness of the Fall throughout the stories of Scripture, from Cain killing Abel (Gen 4), to the Israelites worshiping the golden calf (Exod 32), to the stoning of Stephen (Acts 7:54–60). We hear calls for the people to repent of their sins throughout the prophets (check out Jonah, Amos, and Hosea). We hear the brokenness of people who recognize their sin in King David (Ps 51 is a great example) and the apostle Paul (see Rom 7:21–24). And while we can see so many examples of the brokenness of the Fall through human relationships, in fact, the whole Creation is impacted by the effects of sin: "We know that the whole creation has been groaning as in the pains of childbirth right up

The Metanarrative of Scripture

to the present time."[1] Examples of the pervasiveness of sin run throughout Scripture.

The heart of *Redemption* is seen most clearly in Jesus' death and resurrection, which is told in all four Gospels—this is the whole point of these books! But we see glimpses of God's redeeming work throughout the whole Bible, from lists of all the sacrifices in the book of Leviticus pointing to the need for atonement for sin, to Isaiah's prophesies of the coming Messiah as a suffering servant (see Isa 53, for example). We see illustrations of Redemption all over the stories in Scripture: from God providing a ram to replace Isaac as the sacrifice Abraham was to offer (see Gen 22:1–14), to David killing the giant Goliath to save the Israelites (1 Sam 17), to the stories of Ruth (the whole book of Ruth is a story of Redemption!) and Esther (though God is never mentioned in the book, he is actively at work, intervening to save his people). Examples of Redemption and the hope of a coming Savior run throughout Scripture.

The book of Revelation, at the end of the Bible, might be the most explicit vision of the full *Restoration* that is to come: the book ends with a vision of the destruction of evil and death and the new creation coming. But we can also see examples of Restoration throughout the stories of the Bible—things that are broken being made right again. We see illustrations of Restoration from the story of Esau reaching out in reconciliation after Jacob had stolen his birthright (Gen 33), to the story of King Josiah restoring the temple and rededicating the people to following the Lord (2 Chr 34), to even the story of Jesus healing a man's ear while he is being betrayed and arrested! (See Luke 22:47–53; it's an amazing little detail of Restoration.) So many of Jesus' miracles are stories of Restoration—of bringing health where there was illness, right relationships where there was strife, and life where there was death. Examples of the ways the new creation is breaking through run throughout Scripture!

These examples are just that—examples to help get your imagination going. But I hope you can see some clear illustrations

---

1. Rom 8:22.

here of what I mean. Seeing the bigger storyline of Scripture helps us make sense of the smaller stories and even helps us find our place in the story as God's people.

That whole idea of "our story inside God's story" is both profound and simple at the same time. It is a profound thing to be able to say, "God is the creator of the whole cosmos . . . and the creator of you and me. Though we are sinful and constantly run away from God, he never turns his back on us and never stops loving us. We cannot save ourselves; we need a savior—and thanks be to God that Jesus paid the debt of sin and redeemed all of Creation! God is making all things new, and we are invited to participate in small, human ways in this work of Restoration." At the same time, this is the simplest story of the whole of Scripture: Creation-Fall-Redemption-Restoration. Seeing ourselves as people connected to the big story of Scripture changes the way we read the Bible and the way we understand what the Bible is for.

And for us, as Christian educators? The wondrous, joyful calling we have received is to help our students see the storyline of the big story of Scripture, to invite them to find their story inside of God's story!

In the next few chapters, let's look at each of these four parts of the big story and start to make some applications to the way we think about what it means to be a human being. In the process we'll develop our Christian imagination and come to better understand how we picture what God is doing—both in the Bible and in his world today. My hope is that will set us up to carefully consider the right role of human beings in relationship to technology through the lens of this storyline.

KEY IDEA FROM THIS CHAPTER

The metanarrative of Scripture helps us see how the smaller stories of Scripture connect to the big story and helps us find our place in God's story as well.

The Metanarrative of Scripture

QUESTIONS FOR REFLECTION AND DISCUSSION

1. What do you make of the idea of a metanarrative from Scripture to give shape to a Christian imagination? Is this a new idea for you? A reframing of an idea? An old idea that is being called to mind? Describe your own reaction to the way this concept was laid out in this chapter.

2. Make a technology connection: can you see Creation-Fall-Redemption-Restoration connections to technology?

7

Creation
God Doesn't Make Junk

THE OPENING ACT IN the drama of Scripture is Creation.

From the very first words of Genesis we cannot escape the fact that there is a Creator: "In the beginning God created the heavens and the earth."[1] As we read through Gen 1, we see God's creativity at work in all things; by speaking the cosmos into being, he also declares his rule over all things. He is the sovereign maker and sustainer of everything.

But there is something else that strikes me in Gen 1. Throughout the poetic prose of the exposition of God's creative work, we hear the refrains echo:

> "And God said . . ."
> ". . . and it was so . . ."
> ". . . and there was evening, and there was morning . . ."
> "And God saw that it was good."[2]

---

1. Gen 1:1.

2. Different translations of Gen 1 may use slightly different language, but the poetic refrains similarly echo. This phrasing comes from the New International Version.

Creation

That last refrain is the one that has absolutely captured my imagination. God saw that everything he made was *good*. I want to emphasize that point, because sometimes when I look around at the world around me it's easy to see things as . . . less than good.

But here is the truth: Creation is good! God does not make junk. God makes beautiful things!

We might see problems in the world around us; there certainly is plenty of hurt, brokenness, and tragedy to find. We'll talk more about that in the next chapter. But let's set our imaginations for Creation aright: the goodness of Creation was there at the very beginning, and God is faithful. I believe that this goodness of Creation carries through right to the present and will carry through into the future as well. Al Wolters, a Christian theologian and philosopher, echoes this thought, stating, "In considering the biblical idea of creation . . . we must not for a moment lose sight of the Creator's sovereign activity in originating, upholding, guiding, and ruling his world."[3] If God is sovereign over all things, the goodness of Creation is under his rule and reign and must remain!

Reading on in Gen 1, I am struck by another amazing statement:

> So God created mankind in his own image,
>   in the image of God he created them;
>   male and female he created them.
> God blessed them and said to them, "Be fruitful and increase in number; fill the earth and subdue it. Rule over the fish in the sea and the birds in the sky and over every living creature that moves on the ground."[4]

Perhaps you, like me, are so used to this language that we don't slow down and think about it. But I hope that it also informs your imagination: human beings are *created in the image of God*.

What an incredible thought! *You* are created in the very image of the God who created the cosmos and rules over it all! Just as a mirror reflects the image of my face, human beings reflect

---

3. Wolters's lovely little book *Creation Regained* is an excellent encouragement to take seriously the goodness of Creation. This quote comes from p. 14.

4. Gen 1:27–28.

what their Creator is like. To be sure, the image you see in the mirror is not *you*, and in the same way, we who bear God's image are *not God*. We did not create the world out of nothing or speak it into being. But we do reflect what God is like. For example, Scripture teaches us that God is love; human image-bearers reflect the capacity to be loving, caring, and compassionate. God is wise; human image-bearers reflect this in our capacity for wisdom and reason. God is just; human image-bearers reflect this in our acts of justice and mercy. God is the Creator; human image-bearers reflect this in our own creative capabilities.

God created human beings in his image, and he gave us the task of caring for Creation, reflecting what he is like as we represent God to the Creation. This means we too are created to create within Creation!

There is a "creative potential" that is present in Creation, which means we can develop the Creation, using what God has made to create things too. Wolters describes the ongoing development of Creation this way: "[God] has put an image of himself on the earth with a mandate to continue . . . in the six-day process of development God had formed it and filled it—but not completely. People must now carry on the work of development: by being fruitful they must fill it even more; by subduing it they must form it even more."[5] What an amazing idea: God expects his image-bearers to explore, and discover, and develop all the treasures of Creation. And by using the God-given powers of our imagination, we can innovate, design, construct, and cultivate wonderful things, carrying on in the creative pathway our Creator laid out for us.

Let's sum up the ideas in this depiction of the first act of the storyline of the big story: Creation. God does not make junk. The goodness of Creation carries through from the beginning up to the present, and on throughout the future. Human beings, as image-bearers, can continue to use the goodness of Creation to develop Creation and innovate within it as well. Your imaginative powers are part of how God designed you to function!

---

5. Wolters, *Creation Regained*, 41.

Creation

KEY IDEA FROM THIS CHAPTER

Understanding the goodness of Creation helps us understand the way things are supposed to be and gives us an imagination for our own creative potential as image-bearers of the Creator.

QUESTIONS FOR REFLECTION AND DISCUSSION

1. How do you react to the depiction of Creation in this chapter? What was an affirmation for you? What was a new idea for you? What questions do you have now?

2. Make a technology connection: how might this view of Creation inform your view of technology? Your view of human beings in relation to technology?

8

Fall
Everything Is Actually Awful

IN THE LAST CHAPTER, we explored the goodness of Creation. And while I deeply believe that the goodness of God's design carries through, I suspect that you, like me, look at the world around us and say, "Well, maybe there is a goodness that remains, but I see an awful lot of busted junk."

Now, let's be very clear: *God does not make junk.* So where does this junk come from?

That's an essentially important question to ask, and Scripture again informs our imagination about the way things have developed. Genesis 3 tells the story of the Fall and how Adam and Eve—as representatives of the whole human race—turned away from God in disobedience. That's what we mean by the Fall, after all: there was a break in the relationship between the Creator and the created ones as humans dove headlong into rebellion against God. The sin of Adam and Eve thoroughly derailed things. Through their disobedience, sin entered the picture, and everything is different as a result—not only do we feel a personal sense of guilt, but

Fall

there is a pollution of the goodness of Creation, and everything is miserable as a result.[1]

To that last point, we sometimes talk about sin as something personal. And truly, sin *is* personal; I know that I fall short of the glory of God daily in what I do and say and even think. But it's important to remember that sin is not *just* personal. The touch of sin is pervasive, and it extends far beyond my personal failings. In fact, through the Fall, *all* of Creation was twisted and tarnished. Al Wolters explains the Fall this way, saying:

> We must stress that the Bible teaches plainly that Adam and Eve's fall into sin was not just an isolated act of disobedience, but an event of catastrophic significance for creation as a whole. Not only the whole human race but the whole nonhuman world too was caught up in the train of Adam's failure to heed God's explicit commandment and warning. The effects of sin touch all of creation; no thing is in principle untouched by the corrosive effects of the fall.[2]

This pervasive nature of sin is a very real problem! It means that *everything* is messed up—everything is polluted by sin. Genesis 3:17 includes this explanation of the terrible curse that the Fall brought on the good Creation:

> Cursed is the ground because of you;
>   through painful toil you will eat food from it
>   all the days of your life.[3]

The very *ground* is cursed through Adam and Eve's sin! This idea is reiterated by the apostle Paul in his letter to the Romans: "We know that the whole creation has been groaning as in the pains of childbirth right up to the present time."[4] The whole of Creation is dilapidated, damaged, defaced, and disrupted.

---

1. This idea of sin as "guilt, pollution, and misery" comes from the Dutch theologian, Herman Bavinck, and it appears in several of his writings.
2. Wolters, *Creation Regained*, 53.
3. Gen 3:17b.
4. Rom 8:22.

It is crucial to remember that this is not how things are supposed to be! Sin does not fit in with God's beautiful work in Creation; it is like a stain that we can't scrub out. Creation is blemished in a way that we can't hide and can't eliminate.

We can say that we believe the goodness of Creation is maintained despite the presence of sin in the world. But it can also be hard to see how things are still good when we see the effects of sin everywhere. The good design of Creation is fractured and distorted in every area: art, technology, entertainment, sexuality, emotions, physical health, families, business, religious organizations, governments . . . All things are damaged by the effects of sin, not least of all our relationships with our fellow image-bearers, and even with God himself. Our very imaginations are twisted by the Fall, and this impacts the stories we tell ourselves as well.

Is there any hope? Creation is crying out for help under duress because of the Fall! But thanks be to God; he provided a solution.

KEY IDEA FROM THIS CHAPTER

Understanding the pervasiveness of the Fall helps us understand the brokenness we see all around us in the world and informs imagination about our need for Redemption.

QUESTIONS FOR REFLECTION AND DISCUSSION

1. How do you react to the depiction of the Fall in this chapter? What was an affirmation for you? What was a new idea for you? What questions do you have now?
2. Make a technology connection: how might this view of the Fall inform your view of technology? Your view of human beings in relation to technology?

9

Redemption
Jesus Loves You!

IN THE LAST TWO chapters, we've been focused on the goodness of Creation and the pervasiveness of the Fall. The touch of the Fall was on all the goodness of Creation; the stain and stink of sin pull our attention away from God's good design. What could be done to fix this situation? Here we come to the third act in the big story of Scripture, the heart of the whole matter: Redemption.

This is the good news of the Gospel, after all: the triune God saves the day—sending Jesus, in love, to rescue us!

We image-bearers are the cause of the problem of sin, and we could not possibly save ourselves. We need God to do that! And, thanks be to God, Jesus certainly came to do just that. Jesus' sacrifice perfectly paid the debt of human sin! His work is truly Redemption: we are bought back from slavery to sin and death and thus can live again in right relationships with God, the very thing that was broken in the Fall. The brokenness itself is broken! Death itself dies!

But here's the thing: the implications of this salvation are far more than just saving me from the debt of my sin or you from the debt of your sin. Christ's redeeming work actually breaks the hold

Part III: The Big Story and Why It Matters

of sin on *all* of Creation. Sin dilapidated, damaged, defaced, and disrupted the goodness of Creation; in the work of Redemption the new creation begins breaking through, restoring, repairing, renovating, and renewing all that has been polluted by sin.

Jesus' death and resurrection brings healing and Restoration for all things. Wolters puts it this way: "Through Christ, God determined to 'reconcile to himself *all things*,' [emphasis in original] writes Paul (Col. 1:20) . . . the scope of redemption is as great as the fall; it embraces creation as a whole."[1] Friends, this is good news! Because of Jesus' redeeming work, we have the possibility of new life through him! And more than that, we have hope that all that seems wrong can—and will!—be made right again.

One of my favorite imagined tellings of the story of Redemption comes from C. S. Lewis's amazing allegory, *The Lion, The Witch, and the Wardrobe*. The White Witch, who represents the devil, has enslaved the land of Narnia, making it "always winter, but never Christmas."[2] What a word picture that is, and it echoes for me that sense of the goodness of Creation absolutely twisted by the effects of the Fall. But there are rumors in Narnia that Aslan, the great Lion, who represents Christ in the story, is on the move. The snow begins to melt, indicating that the Witch's hold might not be as complete as we were led to believe!

If you've read the book, I'm sure you can't forget scene at the Stone Table. Here we see Aslan, the great Lion, volunteering to lay down his life in place of the treacherous traitor, Edmund. Allowing himself to be sacrificed on the Stone Table, Aslan willingly takes the place of the one who deserves death, but he cannot remain dead, because of the "deep magic from before the dawn of time."[3]

---

1. Wolters, *Creation Regained*, 72.

2. Lewis, *Lion, the Witch*, 24. The faun, Mr. Tumnus, describes the power of the White Witch this way when Lucy first meets him. This is a powerful, poetic image of the reality of the curse of sin!

3. Chapter 15 in *The Lion, the Witch, and the Wardrobe* dramatically explains this "deep magic"—the witch understood the need for a sacrifice but did not perceive the truth of atonement, which is what this illustration of the breaking of the Table means: the power of sin is broken, and Aslan is alive again!

Redemption

And the Table itself cracks at his resurrection—death itself begins to die! And, in the end, the power of the Witch is fully broken, as she too is destroyed by the great Lion and his victory.

The victory of Aslan over the Witch's power is a powerful illustration of what Redemption looks like, and imagining the Redemption of all things is heart of Lewis's story. Because of Jesus' redeeming work, he has asserted his sovereignty over all things, like Aslan's rule over all of Narnia. The Witch no longer had any claim, and the power of sin in our world is likewise broken.

I think it's important that we recall that Christ's work of Redemption is the beginning of a *Restoration* of things. God does not dump his original Creation to make a different one in response to the effects of sin. He *saves* Creation. Redemption is God's salvage operation! Wolters puts it this way: "He refuses to abandon the work of his hands—in fact he sacrifices his own Son to save his original project. Humankind, which has botched its original mandate and the whole creation along with it, is given another chance in Christ; we are reinstated as God's managers on earth. The original good creation is to be restored."[4] Isn't that a wonderful thought?

In fact, Lewis includes this same impulse at the end of *The Lion, The Witch, and the Wardrobe*. After defeating the Witch and redeeming Narnia from her power, the Lion puts the four children who have been part of the story—"Sons of Adam and Daughters of Eve"[5]—in place to reign in his stead, calling to mind the way that human image-bearers are called to rule over and develop Creation in Gen 1. In our fallen state, we cannot do this work rightly because of sin's tarnishing effects on us. But because of Christ's redeeming work, all is made right, bought back, and reclaimed. The things that were lost have been found. The things that were

---

4. Wolters, *Creation Regained*, 70–71.

5. Lewis uses this term for the human children throughout the book; it is introduced in chapter 2, when Lucy first meets Mr. Tumnus. In the final chapter of the book, we see Aslan installing Peter, Susan, Edmund, Lucy on their thrones as his regents, "sons of Adam and daughters of Eve" rightly living out the human calling to rule over creation.

shattered are repaired. The things that were bent out of shape have been straightened.

To summarize the story so far: God created all things good. Human beings broke relationship with God and plunged the whole world into brokenness. Jesus came to save the day. Now, how shall we live?

KEY IDEA FROM THIS CHAPTER

Understanding the cosmic scope of Christ's Redemption helps us remember that he loves not only us image-bearers but the whole Creation and went to all lengths to salvage what was broken!

QUESTIONS FOR REFLECTION AND DISCUSSION

1. How do you react to the depiction of Christ's redeeming work in this chapter? What was an affirmation for you? What was a new idea for you? What questions do you have now?
2. Make a technology connection: how might this view of Redemption inform your view of technology? Your view of human beings in relation to technology?

10

Restoration
How Then Shall We Live?

THE FOURTH ACT IN the metanarrative of Scripture is Restoration. This is the part of the story where we currently find ourselves! We certainly must keep in mind the Creation, Fall, and Redemption acts, but perhaps this is the part of the story that feels the most immediate for our day-to-day lives.

What does Restoration mean? And what does this mean for how we live our lives today?

I want to first distinguish between Redemption and Restoration. We have to remember that *only* Christ can do the work of Redemption. While we humans were created very good,[1] we are absolutely and totally infected by sin and in need of a Savior. The apostle Paul teaches this need directly, saying, "For all have sinned and fall short of the glory of God, and all are justified freely by his grace through the redemption that came by Christ Jesus."[2] Praise God that Jesus did this redeeming work, because he is the

---

1. Genesis 1:31a describes God looking at his whole Creation after creating his image-bearers, and God says, "God saw all that he had made, and it was very good." You and I are created "very good"!

2. Rom 3:23–24.

sinless one![3] Only one without sin could pay the debt of sin,[4] so only Jesus can redeem.

But what about Restoration? Is that something we image-bearers can do?

I think that Restoration is different than Redemption. Restoration carries the sense of healing what is sick, reconciling what is divided, or repairing what is broken. Certainly, Christ's Redemption sets the conditions where things can be renewed! But this is not a "repristination," a rolling back of the clock to the garden of Eden before the Fall. Restoration takes seriously the idea that God loves this world and that he was willing to sacrifice his Son to salvage it and renovate it.

And here is an incredible truth: through the power of the Holy Spirit, Christ invites us to participate in his Restoration work of healing, reconciliation, and repair. Here is Paul's description of this invitation:

> Therefore, if anyone is in Christ, the new creation has come: The old has gone, the new is here! All this is from God, who reconciled us to himself through Christ and gave us the ministry of reconciliation: that God was reconciling the world to himself in Christ, not counting people's sins against them. And he has committed to us the message of reconciliation. We are therefore Christ's ambassadors, as though God were making his appeal through us.[5]

Notice what Paul says here: God is reconciling the world—all of Creation!—to himself, and he has given *us* the opportunity to

---

3. 2 Corinthians 5:21 says, "God made him who had no sin to be sin for us, so that in him we might become the righteousness of God."

4. Hebrews 7:25–27 says, "Therefore he is able to save completely those who come to God through him, because he always lives to intercede for them. Such a high priest truly meets our need—one who is holy, blameless, pure, set apart from sinners, exalted above the heavens. Unlike the other high priests, he does not need to offer sacrifices day after day, first for his own sins, and then for the sins of the people. He sacrificed for their sins once for all when he offered himself."

5. 2 Cor 5:17–20a.

again be ambassadors to the whole Creation, just like his original calling to humans back in Gen 1. The difference in language here between "ruling over" Creation and having a "message of reconciliation" to the world strikes me as important. We represent Christ to this world, but we don't do the redeeming work. We bear witness to the new creation!

I think it's worth remembering that we are living in the "in-between times" now. Jesus has already fought the decisive battle at the cross, and the defeat of the power of sin and death and evil is sure. And yet, the war rages on, even though the final victory has already been soundly assured. We, Jesus' redeemed people, are welcomed to join in the fight as well.[6] But as soon as I say that, I think we must be clear about what this "fight" truly looks like. Christ has already won the battle, after all! And so, our role takes on an entirely different character: we "fight" by living out the fruit of the Spirit: love, joy, peace, patience, kindness, faithfulness, gentleness, and self-control.[7] We are fighting for renewal, reconciliation, and Restoration.

At the risk of deflating your ego, we need to remember that Jesus does not need us. He is God, after all! Rather, he loves us and *invites* us to participate in the renewal of all things. And this invitation makes all the difference for us in understanding how we should live as his redeemed people!

KEY IDEA FROM THIS CHAPTER

Understanding the role of human beings—God's image-bearers—in the work of Restoration helps us understand how we should live as redeemed people.

---

6. Wolters uses this analogy of wartime between Jesus and the forces of evil—how Jesus has really spelled out their doom, and is now moving toward the mopping-up operation to great effect on pp. 83–86 of *Creation Regained*.

7. Gal 5:27–28.

Part III: The Big Story and Why It Matters

QUESTIONS FOR REFLECTION AND DISCUSSION

1. How do you react to the depiction of Restoration as healing, reconciling, or repairing as described in this chapter? What was an affirmation for you? What was a new idea for you? What questions do you have now?

2. Make a technology connection: how might this view of Restoration inform your view of technology? Your view of human beings in relation to technology?

11

Becoming a Truth-Seeker
Navigating Competing Stories

IN THE PAST FEW chapters, we've been exploring the big story of Scripture: Creation-Fall-Redemption-Restoration. I hope that this has been a boost for you; to think carefully and deeply about how the four Acts of this big story drama can illustrate the contours of a Christian imagination. I'm also hoping that we can use that metanarrative of Scripture to help us address the big questions and concerns we have when it comes to innovation and the development of new technologies.

The challenge is, we often find ourselves in the midst of competing stories. We need a way of orienting ourselves to discern the truth. And I think the big story can be a useful and effective way to make sense of the stories we find ourselves in.

For example, when it comes to the role of artificial intelligence in education, I think there are several competing stories that educators might sense—each of which might have some truth to them.

One story is the "incorporating innovation" story. In this story, we see the awesome potential of artificial intelligence. AI can transform what is possible for our teaching, and even for our students' learning, so why wouldn't we use it? It can make us more productive, freeing up time from the low-level tasks of teaching to prioritize opportunities for connection with students, emphasizing relationships and personalizing our teaching to give each student just what he or she needs to flourish and thrive. With all this potential, it almost seems sinful to *not* embrace innovation!

But hold on a second, because there is another story we might see—one that directly competes with this first story. This second story is the "policing problems" story. In this story, we can clearly see the challenges that new technologies bring. We develop carefully constructed learning opportunities for students and assign them what we see as meaningful, valuable work that will help them learn and grow. But students often don't see the importance of the hard work and instead short-circuit their own learning by using AI to complete the assignment. In this case, educators need to regulate students' use of technology to ensure that they are actually doing their own work, to keep them on track and truly learning. The technology gets in the way of scholarly opportunities, and we might be tempted to ban the use of these powerful tools.

And then there might be a third story we can see—a different approach altogether, compared to these first two tales. This third story is the "ostrich option" story. This is a tale of being overwhelmed and overtaxed; educators already have so many things they need to do on a daily basis, and we might want to just say "Jesus, take the wheel!" It might be true that there are benefits from using AI, and it might be true that students might misuse it, but it's all just too much for us to take on. So instead, we trust that the Lord will sort it all out, and we take the ostrich approach of hiding our head in the sand, whether because we are fearful of being found to be inadequate with our knowledge and skill when it comes to AI or because we feel overburdened by the to-do list of other pressing tasks.

Here's the thing, friends: I think that these three stories each actually have some alignment with the big story of Scripture! The "incorporating innovation" story sees the creative potential of technology, aligning most clearly with the Creation movement of the big story. The "policing problems" story sees the results of the Fall in full force. And the "ostrich option" story—believe it or not—might connect with the Redemption act, relying on Jesus' work to make things right that seem out of our control. There are elements of the truth in each of these stories and connections with the metanarrative of the Bible in each one.

However, each of these reduces the *whole* story to just *part* of the story. And here is where we need the wisdom of a fully formed Christian imagination! Because each of these stories only has part of the whole truth, we need to take seriously the *whole story*. Creation—and human creative potential—is an important part of the story. The Fall—and the way all things are twisted because of sin—is an important part of the story. Redemption—Christ's work, that we humans cannot do—is (clearly!) an important part of the story. And we are right to take all of these parts of the story seriously. But we need to take the *whole* story seriously.

This is messy, isn't it? Embracing the whole story means we are working to discern the whole truth, even when it seems potentially contradictory. Each movement of the big story helps us see the truth more fully. God created all things good. Human sinfulness twisted everything. Jesus came to save the day. We are invited to work toward the Restoration of all things.

When it comes to big, complex issues like "what should we do about AI in education?" we need to have a bigger story—the biggest story!—to help us orient ourselves to the truth and find ourselves in a better story in the process.

KEY IDEA FROM THIS CHAPTER

We often find ourselves in competing stories, and the big story of Scripture can help us orient ourselves to discern truth.

Part III: The Big Story and Why It Matters

QUESTIONS FOR REFLECTION AND DISCUSSION

1. As you read the three stories (incorporating innovation, policing problems, and the ostrich option), did you gravitate more to one of them as opposed to the others? Which one, and why? And if not, why not?

2. There wasn't a Restoration-oriented story included in this chapter. What might an incomplete "Restoration" story look like?

PART IV

Demystifying Artificial Intelligence

12

Thoughts on Intelligence
Should We Be Worried About "Actual Stupidity"?

I WAS RECENTLY TALKING with a friend about the reading and exploring I've been doing with various forms of AI. He joked in response, "Everyone is talking about 'artificial intelligence.' But I'm more worried about 'actual stupidity.'" That's a good line, isn't it? Honestly, I think this point is well made. There seems to be more than enough foolishness and ignorance to go around amongst human beings before we even begin to think about artificial forms of intelligence!

His quip got me thinking quite a bit about intelligence and just what we mean by "artificial intelligence." What does it mean to be "intelligent," anyway? And do machines have some capacity for intelligence? Here again, you probably already have an imagination for intelligence and an imagination for whether machines have intelligence.

Take Clippy, for example. Clippy was an animated paperclip in an early version of Microsoft Word. It was a sort of early artificial intelligence agent, designed to try and help you with your writing. If you started a new document and began writing, "Dear Grandma

Part IV: Demystifying Artificial Intelligence

. . ." Clippy would spring into action, dancing in the corner of the screen, with a text box that would pop up: "Hey there! It looks like you might be trying to write a letter. Would you like me to help?" And Clippy would suggest some templates that you might use for your letter to your grandmother.

Sounds like a helpful addition to a word processor, doesn't it? Unfortunately, there were two major problems this supposedly intelligent agent. First, Clippy was *annoying*. Users almost always immediately closed Clippy's pop-ups, rather than actually using them. And this reveals the second problem: Clippy was *not helpful*. Most of Clippy's suggestions did not seem all that intelligent, because they were either painfully obvious or linked to an obscure feature in Word that you were almost certainly *not* trying to use. So just how intelligent is an annoying, unhelpful agent? Most users answer, "not very intelligent!"

But Clippy is just a particularly clear example of an unhelpful implementation of AI. The truth is, you almost certainly have been using AI on an almost daily basis for years now, and you probably find AI to be a very helpful, very useful part of your life. And when I say you've been using AI for years, I suspect this has been true for you *long* before you ever heard of AI chatbots like ChatGPT. Here are just a few examples:

- Autocorrect, predictive text, and speech-to-text on your phone are all powered by artificial intelligence.
- So are recommendation engines on streaming platforms like Netflix or Spotify.
- As are search engine algorithms that help you find the thing you're actually looking for online.
- Personal digital assistants (think Siri or Alexa) are great examples of using artificial intelligence to make sense of your voice input and giving an appropriate response.
- Ever use facial recognition—perhaps to unlock your phone? That's AI-powered as well.

Thoughts on Intelligence

- Ever use a map app to help plan a route for a trip? You guessed it—powered by AI.
- Even the mundane tools built into your word processor like spellcheck and grammar check—all powered by artificial intelligence.

Truly, AI has very likely been part of your life for the better part of a decade by now.

Now, you might say, "But those are pretty 'unintelligent' uses of AI. Generative AI—like AI chatbots—seems much more . . . intelligent." And I would tend to agree with you; it *seems* much more intelligent. But this is also part of our imagination for what the AI is actually doing when we prompt it and see a response.

Our imagination for what AI is and how it works—and what it actually means to be "intelligent"—might be flawed. We think we understand intelligence, but I am not sure you and I have an accurate assessment of what we really mean by the word "intelligence."

I've heard the human brain described this way: "If your brain was simple enough that you could understand it, you would be too simple to understand it." And while we have made great strides in neuroscience to understand the structures and functions of the human brain, human beings still have many questions about thinking, memory, learning, forgetting, and the difference between our brains and our minds. I again want to call back Andy Crouch's definition of what it means to be human: "Every human person is a heart-soul-mind-strength complex designed for love."[1] We certainly cannot be reduced to our minds. But we also are not fully human without our minds. And our minds function in concert with our hearts, souls, and bodies, and all of these together designed for loving God and others.

Taken in this light, I think there is something quite profoundly different between human intelligence and the "intelligence" of machines. In the next few chapters, we'll try to come to understand what artificial intelligence is and how it works. But I want

---

1. Crouch, *Life We're Looking For*, 33.

you to hold in mind (ha!) this important point: human intelligence is *fundamentally* different than "artificial intelligence."

KEY IDEA FROM THIS CHAPTER

Artificial intelligence is useful but fundamentally different from human intelligence—and we might not fully understand human intelligence in the first place!

QUESTIONS FOR REFLECTION AND DISCUSSION

1. When you hear that quip about being more worried about "actual stupidity," what comes to mind for you? Did you first think about machines? Or people? What might that illustrate about your imagination?

2. What do you make of the claim that the "intelligence" of machines is fundamentally different than the intelligence of human beings? Do you agree? Disagree? What does your response to this prompt illustrate about your imagination for AI?

13

Understanding AI—How Do Computers Work?

I AM NOT A "car guy." I have friends who are—the sort of folks who can tell you all the details about a given production year for a particular make and model. They can talk engine volumes, RPMs, wheel sizes, and body types, and it starts to sound a bit like gibberish to me. I don't know all the details about how cars work. But I know how to drive, and I know enough to be able to check the oil, add windshield wiper fluid, and discern what the light that just lit up on the dashboard display means. I'm not a car guy, but I know enough.

In a similar way, I hope that this chapter and the next few will give you a little introduction to how AI chatbots actually work. But this isn't going to be a "car guy" discussion—it's going to be an "add wiper fluid" level of explanation, okay? I think that to get the most out of what AI can (and cannot!) do for us as educators, we should become comfortable with popping the hood and having a look at the engine compartment. So, let's give it a whirl, shall we?

Let's start by talking about what a computer is. This might sound silly, but let's begin with the idea that a computer is a device that *computes*. At the simplest level, all a computer really does is handle data by taking some data as input, processing the data in

Part IV: Demystifying Artificial Intelligence

some way, and reporting the output data. That isn't all that different from a basic calculator, right? You punch in some numbers (input), the calculator does the math functions you ask for (processing), and you see the result on a little screen (output). Fundamentally, this is what a computer is doing: input, processing, output.

Computer scientists would call this the black box model of computing—the machine accepts input, conducts some processes, and then outputs something. From the user's perspective, processing is the black box—we know something happens, but we don't know how it works. It's kind of like how I know that my car has an engine, and there are things happening under the hood, but I don't know all the details; I just trust that the engine will work and my car will get me from point A to point B. But the idea that I can use the car to get from point A to point B is a really important one: context matters for how I use my car, like knowing my starting location and the place I want to end up.

Similarly, computers need to be told what "matters" for the computing that they do. Let me give you two examples to help illustrate what I mean by context.[1]

1. Can you read the following sentence? *Ths sntnc hs th vwls mssng.* If you could make sense of it, you are not a computer. A computer needs to be told what matters, like the use of vowels. Your brain functions differently; you are able to use context to make sense of things, even if you don't have all the data given to you.

2. Consider these three questions:

    - How much information is there in five hundred pages of Tolkien's *Lord of the Rings*?

    - How much information is there in a five-hundred-page phone book?

---

[1]. My friend, Kari Sandouka, who is a professor of computer science, uses these examples in her Introduction to Software Engineering course to help programmers understand information processing.

Understanding AI—How Do Computers Work?

- How much information is there in a ream of five hundred blank sheets of printer paper?

If you are thinking something like "that is a ridiculous question!" you are probably not a computer. You know that what is *on* those five hundred pages really makes a big difference for how much information there is! But a computer needs to be told the context, or else a page is a page is a page.

All of this is to say that your brain and a computer function in very different ways!

I want to start here because it's important to keep in mind that while computers—including the ones that run AI chatbots—are very powerful machines, what they really do is process data. They receive input. They process that data. They generate output. They don't really "think," at least not in the way we consider human thinking. And while some folks call the processor the "brain" of the computer, I want us to be specific in *not* describing it that way. This is part of having a better imagination for what the computer is actually doing when it is "thinking" and "learning."

I also want to be very clear that I think that computers are incredibly helpful tools! But we must be careful about treating them as magical in some way. Andy Crouch makes this argument—about technology feeling "magical"—in a profound way:

> The dream is that human beings could acquire the ultimate superpower: the ability to do magic. We no longer call it by that name, to be sure. Instead, we call it technology. But as the science fiction author Arthur C. Clarke famously observed, "Any sufficiently advanced technology is indistinguishable from magic." The quality that delights and intoxicates us in our technological devices is the way they promise to work without us, without asking very much of us—like magic.[2]

The truth of Crouch's argument hits close to home for me. The more powerful the devices, the more magical they seem. And

---

2. Crouch, *Life We're Looking For*, 60–61. The chapter this quote is from is all about understanding the ancient roots of our (misguided) human quest to make "magic" a reality.

today's computers *are* powerful devices; the smartphone I carry around in my pocket is *far* more powerful than the computers that NASA used to send humans to the moon in the 1960s, and I carry it around without any thought to how formidable it really is. And at the same time, I want that smartphone to magically give me superpowers—to let me document and record every activity so I will never forget anything, to allow me to tap into the sum of human knowledge, to help me broadcast my thoughts to the world, and more.

At its root, though, my smartphone—and all other computing devices—are just powerful calculators, taking data as input, processing that data, and providing an output. It's a good reminder for us all to not imagine our computers as something more than they actually are, as if they can "think" the way we do.

KEY IDEA FROM THIS CHAPTER

Computers—even very powerful computers!—do not "think" in the same way humans think. Computers are machines that compute: they receive input data, process it in a specified way, and report an output.

QUESTIONS FOR REFLECTION AND DISCUSSION

1. Based on what you read in this chapter, does it make sense to describe the "thinking" done by humans and by computers as very different things? Why or why not?
2. Check your imagination: think through the Creation-Fall-Redemption-Restoration metanarrative. How do the ideas from this chapter connect with the big story?

14

Neural Networks
More Powerful Processing

IN THE LAST CHAPTER, we explored how computers actually work—they receive data as input, process that data in a specified way, and generate an output. I suggested that I believe this is quite different than how human beings think. We sometimes describe human thinking as "processing," and we sometimes talk about machines handling data as "thinking," but it seems to me that these are really quite different things. If you think about your own brain and how it functions, you might be able to see this difference starkly.

The way computers typically work is that they handle data sequentially. They work step-by-step as they process data, moving from inputs to outputs and then receiving new inputs to generate new outputs in a cycle that continues until the program is complete. But this step-by-step processing architecture is not the only way to devise a computer.

Neurons are nerve cells that carry signals throughout your body—and especially within your brain. On one end of the neuron are many branching structures called dendrites, looking a little like the branches of a tree. Dendrites receive signals from other nerve cells, and send them on through the neuron. On the other end of the neuron there is a long single fiber that extends out of the cell body of the neuron called an axon. The axon can carry the signal a long way through the brain and then transmits the signal to the dendrite of another neuron. The key thing is that dendrites can receive signals from many different neurons, and axons can connect to dendrites of multiple dendrites of other neurons. When you are thinking, nerve signals move from neuron to neuron in a complex pattern, with the signals running from the dendrites of one neuron down the axon to the dendrites of another neuron. And when you learn something new, you make a new connection between two neurons. But this is quite different than the way the tiny switches inside a computer's processor make the calculations they are doing as they process data.

I wanted to take this little foray into neuroscience to be clear about how human brain cells function and what learning looks at a cellular level in human brains, because there are a few terms that get tossed around when we start learning a bit about how AI chatbots work. Terms like "neural networks," "machine learning," and "large language models" sound like phrases out of science fiction, don't they? Maybe they are part of your imagination for AI because of science fiction stories you've heard or watched? Let's demystify them a bit, because they get at another way of structuring a computer beyond the typical step-by-step architecture we have been thinking about so far.

A neural network is a kind of computer architecture with a design inspired by the way neurons are connected in a human brain. While a more standard computer architecture processes data in a linear step-by-step format, in a neural network, there are multiple pathways working at the same time to process data simultaneously. But I want to be clear that when I say this architecture is inspired by neurons in a human brain, it still doesn't function quite the same way your neurons do when you are thinking.

If we think of dendrites as the "input" side of a neuron and an axon as the "output" side of a neuron, there is an analogy to devising a computer that we can make for a neural network approach. Like the many branching dendrites in a human neuron, there are

Neural Networks

multiple "input" pathways into a neural network. And like the way an axon can connect to multiple other neurons, there are also multiple "output" possibilities for a neural network. There are multiple processors that are functioning in parallel, similar to the way multiple neurons can be conducting signals simultaneously in your brain. The image below illustrates what this looks like.

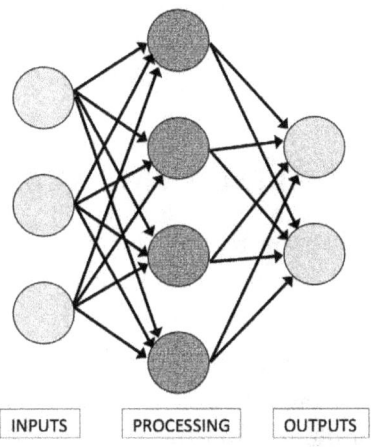

Image by David Mulder.

I again want to encourage you to check your imagination of what is happening here. While it's true that the neural network provides for more powerful processing of data because there are multiple pathways working simultaneously, the fundamental action is still very similar to the linear, step-by-step processing we were considering earlier: input, processing, output. It is certainly true that this kind of architecture allows for more data to be handled simultaneously, which means things can happen faster—though almost certainly requiring more energy to make these calculations more rapidly as well. And this more powerful processing is what allows for more powerful—and "magical"—AI programs to run.

The key question we still need to consider is this: "Is the machine *thinking*?" When compared to the human brain, even using this neural network architecture, I think the answer is "not thinking like a human." And if it's not thinking like a human, can we

Part IV: Demystifying Artificial Intelligence

describe the machine as *learning* like a human? That's where we're headed in the next chapter.

KEY IDEA FROM THIS CHAPTER

Neural networks are a type of computer architecture that are inspired by the way neurons are connected in the human brain and can allow for faster data processing, which is key for more powerful AI programs to be able to run efficiently.

QUESTIONS FOR REFLECTION AND DISCUSSION

1. Based on what you read in this chapter, how well does a computer's processing mirror human thinking? Do you find yourself drawing a contrast between "processing" and "thinking"? Why or why not?

2. Check your imagination: think through the Creation-Fall-Redemption-Restoration metanarrative. How do the ideas from this chapter connect with the big story?

15

Machine Learning and Probability
Basic Ideas for Programming AI

WE LEFT OFF IN the last chapter discussing neural networks and whether the processing done by this type of computer is akin to human thinking. Neural networks provide for much faster processing of data because there are multiple inputs and multiple processors leading to multiple outputs as well. And it is true that the human brain can handle multiple signals traveling rapidly concurrently; with the billions of neurons in your brain, you have billions of impulses being sent every second!

But questions remain about just how similar a computer's processing truly is to human thinking. And more than that, the question of whether a machine can truly *learn* is a really interesting one to think about. The term *machine learning* is another one we need to consider to develop understanding about what is happening with generative AI.

When you learn something new, you make a connection between two neurons in your brain. The axon of one neuron becomes associated with the dendrite of another neuron, and the more you think about that new thing you've learned, the more you strengthen the connection. The old saying in neuroscience is "neurons that fire together wire together." This means that repeated practice can strengthen understanding by strengthening the connection between those neurons. Something kind of similar happens in machine learning, but it is much more based on probability than this kind of association between dendrites and axons in the human brain.

Machine learning is a way of developing a piece of software by training a computer program to be able to compare and contrast to "learn" a concept. Let's say you want to train your program to identify a car. How would you go about doing this? One effective technique is to use examples and non-examples of cars to build a database of "car" and "not car" for the program to draw upon. A picture of a Ford Mustang? That's a car! A picture of a baby duck? Nope, not a car. A picture of a Toyota Corolla? Car. A picture of a windmill? Not a car. Volkswagen Beetle? Car. Actual beetle? Not a car. You get the idea? After hundreds or thousands or millions of examples, the program has a large database to draw upon to be able to recognize a car.

As an aside, you might be wondering how this training actually takes place. This sort of training is done by humans who identify the examples and non-examples to provide the database for the program. In fact, all those CAPTCHA images you've had to click on over the years to prove you are a human being have been used by big technology companies to help train their AI programs by machine learning. (You know, those things that say "click on all the pictures of boats" or "click on all the pictures of elephants" or things like that? You were almost certainly helping to develop a machine learning algorithm.)

Okay, back to our example of machine learning: trying to figure out what a "car" is. Now that you have a program that can determine what a car is, will it get it right all the time? Unfortunately, no. Big data certainly helps: the larger the dataset, the better the program's ability to judge whether something is a car. But the *quality* of the data is also very important; the old saying in computer science is "garbage in, garbage out," which means we don't just need a lot of data—we need "good" data. So, there is usually

Machine Learning and Probability

further fine-tuning that must happen with human guidance—giving specific feedback to correct for errors and refine the program's ability to differentiate.

Let's further imagine we wanted to refine our car-detection program by teaching it to identify a taxi as a particular kind of car. Can you imagine the further tuning that would need to happen? The program can already determine if something is a car, but it would take some human input to guide the software into being able to correctly identify a car as a taxi. For instance, in the US, taxis are often yellow, but this is not universally true—taxis are often black in the UK, and even in the US, taxis can be other colors. There would have to be more specific refinement beyond even the color of the car. For the program to "learn" to identify a taxi as a particular kind of car there is going to be a process of building up the database that the program can draw from as it makes calculations to determine the likelihood that a car is a taxi.

Imagine that you have a picture of a yellow car that you feed into our taxi-identifying program. How likely is it that the new example of a yellow car is a taxi? The program will pass this data on to the neural network (input), which will calculate the probability (processing the data) that the car is a taxi by comparing it to items in the database. After making a probability calculation, it will report (output) whether or not the car is a taxi. And then, a human judge will almost certainly have to give some fine-tuning to confirm that the machine is correct . . . or feedback that it is incorrect, which the program will include as an update to the database so it will be able to make a better prediction next time.

Machine learning, then, uses similarity measures as a key aspect for making a judgment about new information—"How likely is it that this is similar to that?" And this is why a neural network is beneficial: the multiple parallel pathways that the computer can use with multiple inputs and multiple processors can help the process of checking the new information against the existing data in the database that has been flagged with as "taxi" or "car but not taxi." If the database is large enough—I'm talking really, really humongous amounts of data to compare against—some impressive results might begin to materialize. And that's what we'll consider in the next chapter.

KEY IDEA FROM THIS CHAPTER

Machine learning is a way of developing a computer program based on examples and non-examples to build up a database. The program that is developed calculates the probability that a new input matches information in the database, which is further fine-tuned by humans to give more accurate outputs over time.

QUESTIONS FOR REFLECTION AND DISCUSSION

1. Based on what you read in this chapter, how well does machine learning replicate human learning? Do you find yourself drawing a contrast between human learning and machine learning? Why or why not?

2. Check your imagination: think through the Creation-Fall-Redemption-Restoration metanarrative. How do the ideas from this chapter connect with the big story?

16

Large Language Models
Generating Responses to Your Prompts

THESE PAST FEW CHAPTERS have been about "poking around under the hood" of what AI programs are doing. To recap, we began by looking at what computers actually do: take input, process the data, and provide an output. We then considered neural networks as a more powerful way to process data with multiple inputs, processors, and potential outputs. And most recently we learned about machine learning and how a large database of examples and non-examples allows humans to train a program to use probability to determine the best output.

Following on the trajectory we've been pursuing, let's now turn our attention to one more key term we need to consider: *large language models*. A large language model is what we are really talking about when we think about generative AI like ChatGPT, Gemini, or Claude, or any of the newer AI chatbots that have popped up recently—these programs are usually called "models" by computer scientists. And a large language model is precisely that: a model (a program) developed using machine learning and an immensely large body of text to train the software to work with human language. This is really the "magic" of a generative AI chatbot: you can give it a prompt in natural, human language as the input. The model uses a neural network to quickly process the data in multiple pathways simultaneously. And the output is again given in natural, human language, based on the massive database it has access to behind the scenes.

When I say a "massive database," I mean incredibly, ridiculously, almost incomprehensibly enormous, like "all of Wikipedia," or even "as much of the Internet as was publicly available in 2022." Imagine the possibilities of being able to draw that much possible information for making those probability-based computations, and you have some idea of why a neural network is required for this kind of data processing—it's a lot of information to work with!

Let's pick on ChatGPT as an example for a moment, because as I'm writing this, it's perhaps the most well-known generative AI chatbot. ChatGPT is an AI-powered chatbot developed by OpenAI, an organization that started as a non-profit but has since morphed into a very valuable technology company. You might wonder about the name "ChatGPT"—why did they call it that? GPT stands for "generative pre-trained transformer." Let's take those three terms in reverse order.

A "transformer" is another name for a neural network—that type of computing architecture we've been thinking about that has multiple pathways for processing data. A transformer allows multiple inputs and multiple processors to handle complex data more efficiently than step-by-step processor designs.

"Pre-trained" means that it is developed using machine learning with human guidance for fine-tuning. Early editions of ChatGPT were developed with a lot of human input. Later editions seem to use more machine learning building on top of these early editions, and there is still plenty of human fine-tuning that goes into refining the program.

That last word, "generative," is the one we need to talk some more about. In a nutshell, this means that the model uses probability to guess what the next best word is, because it takes its input in human language, and it puts its output likewise into human language. The output is generated by the transformer, based on the information in the large language model's database.

What actually happens when you type a prompt into the text box for an AI chatbot? The input for the program is in plain English (or Spanish, or Russian, or whatever other languages the chatbot can take as input). The large language model takes advantage of parallel processing to calculate the probability of the next word, and the output is generated word-by-word based on that probability.

What I mean by "generated by probability" probably warrants an example to illustrate. Imagine we are going to ask the chatbot to just predict the final word of this sentence: "The dog likes to sleep in her ___." What word should fill in the blank? The chatbot searches its database for example words that could fill in this blank. In the database there are lots of possible words that could be used, and the model uses the power of the neural network to check lots of possibilities. The chatbot then calculates the probability of which of these possible words is the "correct" output based on the way words are associated within the database.

So, for our example, let's say the chatbot finds some possibilities for filling in the blank: "bag," "bed," "box," and "buttons." Which of these do you think is most likely? As the chatbot checks the database, it finds very few examples of dogs sleeping in buttons, so the probability of this response is ranked very low. There are a few examples of dogs sleeping in bags and more examples of dogs sleeping in boxes, so these are ranked as higher probability. But there are a lot of examples of dogs sleeping in beds, so the probability of this word being "correct" is ranked the highest. All these calculations happen in the blink of an eye, and the chatbot gives the output: "The dog likes to sleep in her bed." As the human judge of this output, you would probably nod your head and agree that this result makes sense. (Conversely, if the chatbot responded "the dog likes to sleep in her buttons," you would probably be confused and think something was amiss with the chatbot!)

This is a simple example, of course. This one probably doesn't feel very magical, does it? Especially when compared to a complex prompt that results in a complex response being generated—it can be a little overwhelming to see what the AI can put together. But it's important to keep in mind that what a generative AI chatbot program is doing, whether in response to a simple prompt or a complex one, is basically the same: it is using the *massive* dataset it has been trained on to play a probability-driven word association game. The program begins by processing the language in the prompt and checking how the words in the prompt are connected in its database. The program then predicts what the "right" words are by checking probabilities of how likely words are to be connected to each other. The program then starts generating a response by adding one word at a time, constantly checking the probability that it is giving the "right" next word. This "predict, choose, add, check" process continues until the program determines it has successfully met the requirement of the prompt.

The results can feel magical, but it truly isn't magic. It's probability.

KEY IDEA FROM THIS CHAPTER

AI chatbots are computer programs known as large language models—programs that are trained on massive, language-based datasets to make probability-based predictions about how to connect words to generate a response to a prompt from a user.

QUESTIONS FOR REFLECTION AND DISCUSSION

1. Based on what you read in this chapter, how does a large language model use probability to generate a response? Does this seem similar to the way human beings create things? Why or why not?

2. Check your imagination: think through the Creation-Fall-Redemption-Restoration metanarrative. How do the ideas from this chapter connect with the big story?

17

Garbage In, Garbage Out
Learning to Talk to a Computer

ONE OF THE OLDEST adages in computer science is "garbage in, garbage out." The idea here is that the machine just does what it is programmed to do: if you get output you don't like or didn't expect, the first place to check is the input you fed into the machine. Computers truly can be frustrating: we expect them to work in particular ways, and sometimes they simply don't do what we expected. But how often are the results actually truly "correct," based on the (faulty) inputs from us poor humans? The reality is that we generally get *exactly* the results we should, because the program, if it is functioning correctly, simply takes the input, processes it accordingly, and feeds us the output.

The caveat "if it is functioning properly" is an important one. So much of the internal process of an AI agent is hidden from us. Honestly, there is a lot of mystery in the functioning of large language models, and even the programmers who develop and train the models have admitted that they don't fully understand how the programs actually work.[1] You may have also heard of AI "hal-

---

1. Sam Altman, the CEO of OpenAI (which is the company behind ChatGPT), has famously admitted that their computer scientists do not fully

lucinations"—situations when the AI seems to be making things up out of thin air. These hallucinations are a real problem: because the program is making associations based on probability, there are situations when the machine calculates the probability incorrectly, leading to misleading, or downright incorrect, results that the AI confidently presents as factual and correct. These hallucinations are an ongoing challenge that AI developers and researchers continue to work to understand and address.[2]

So how can we get the best results from our AI-powered tools? I have two broad suggestions to consider. First, we need to learn to write better prompts that will help us get the output we are looking for. Second, we need to approach the AI-powered tools as an eager assistant that will almost certainly need some redirection—which means our work with the AI will be an iterative process of trying a few things in sequence. Tinkering will help you discover some strategies that are more effective to get the desired results.

Here's an approach I've found helpful for writing better prompts—it's one I've co-opted from the guru of differentiated instruction, Carol Ann Tomlinson.[3] The strategy is called RAFT, and while it works great for creating differentiated assignments for students, it also has proven to be a really effective approach

---

understand how ChatGPT generates the results it outputs and has described the functioning of large language models as a black box. This is an intriguing—and troubling—prospect: the folks creating these powerful tools are not entirely sure how they work! See Tangerman, "Sam Altman Admits," for the whole story.

2. Sal Khan, the founder of Khan Academy and proponent of Khanmigo, the personal AI tutor the company is developing, admits the challenges of developing AI that doesn't hallucinate as it generates responses. His book *Brave New Words* explains some of this development and the ways they are working to mitigate hallucinations by feeding very specific data into their models database and developing safeguards to ensure students get the best data possible.

3. Tomlinson's 2003 book *Fulfilling the Promise of the Differentiated Classroom* was an absolute game-changer for the way I approached tailoring instruction to the needs of different kids in my class, and it's packed with practical, realistic ideas for adjusting the processes, products, and even content to be learned to make learning meaningful and accessible for students. The general approach of RAFT I'm sharing in this chapter comes from pp. 133–35 of the book.

for me to write better prompts for my AI-assisted projects. RAFT is an acronym for Role, Audience, Format, and Topic. Using this strategy for writing a prompt means you have to tell the AI chatbot to take on a particular role and give it a particular audience that the work will be used for. Then carefully construct the format you expect for the output. Finally, give the necessary details of the topic for the work.

What does this look like in practice? Let's look at two examples.

1. Imagine that you are going to use the AI chatbot to help you write an email to parents about an upcoming class trip to a science museum. Note the specific details in the prompt about role, audience, format, and topic:

   > I am a middle school science teacher and I am writing an email to the parents and guardians of my seventh-grade students to inform them about an upcoming class trip to the science museum. Compose a professionally worded email that explains that this trip is an opportunity to make connections to things we have been learning in science class this year. Remind them that students will need to pack a lunch for the trip, and include the fact that we are still looking for three volunteers to help chaperone this trip. Make the whole message not more than two hundred words in length.

2. Imagine that you are going to use the AI chatbot to help you create a rubric that you will use to give feedback on an essay that you are assigning to your students. Again, note the specific details about the role, audience, format, and topic:

   > I am a fourth-grade classroom teacher, and I am teaching my students to write a five-paragraph persuasive essay. I am creating a rubric I will use to give feedback to my students on their essays. Create a rubric that describes four levels of achievement for each of these criteria: Clear thesis statement, Supporting evidence, Recap of key ideas,

Powerful argument, Careful grammar and punctuation. Make the four levels of achievement: "Wow!," "Good Work," "In Progress . . .," and "Getting Started."

The specificity of these prompts makes it more likely that you'll get the kind of result you're hoping for in the output, but it's not guaranteed. This is what I mean about the "tinkering" aspect of developing your prompt for the AI—it might take more than one attempt. But as you continue to experiment and explore, your results will likely become better as you become a more proficient prompter.

Here's an example of that kind of refinement in action. Remember the story I told in the opening chapter of this book, where I shared about my friend Jon telling me about his website and I responded with "what is a website?" I prompted ChatGPT to create an image recreating that picture of Jon that came up on my computer screen the first time I was on the World Wide Web.

Here is the prompt I initially gave ChatGPT to create an illustration: "Create an image of a college student playing a guitar in his dorm room." It's a straightforward prompt, and I got a pretty good result: a picture of a clean-cut kid wearing glasses with an acoustic guitar, sitting on a bed, with a poster and a pennant labeled "college" hanging on the wall in the background. Not bad at all, really.

However, this image looks *nothing* like the photo of Jon I saw on my computer screen in 1995. So, I revised my initial prompt to make it much more specific: "Create an image of a college-age white male approximately twenty 20 years old playing an acoustic guitar in his dorm room. He should be wearing a blue and yellow tie-dyed T-shirt and black shorts. He should have a goatee and mustache and have wavy, shoulder-length, brown hair that looks like it is in motion as he plays. Make him look like he is playing quite energetically—really rocking out!"

And the result? Well, you don't know my friend Jon, but the image I got looks an awful lot like he did in the mid-1990s! Tie-dyed T-shirt, a mop of hair in motion, and singing his heart out as he played his guitar: that's my buddy, Jon, as generated by the AI in response to a detailed prompt.

Garbage In, Garbage Out

This is the power of crafting a careful prompt—you're much more likely to get the result you're looking for! We have to remember what the AI is actually doing: it's a computer program that is taking the input we give it, processing the data, and using probability to figure out the "right" result. If we aren't happy with the result, rethinking the input we give the program is a good first step. Tinkering with the way you phrase your prompt can almost always get you a better outcome, more closely aligned with what you are imaging the AI program will generate. This demands a bit of a playful approach, but I have definitely found that being a little playful in your prompting—and being more specific about what you want the AI to do—will make much more likely that you'll find a satisfying result.

KEY IDEA FROM THIS CHAPTER

The way we prompt AI directly impacts the result, and taking time to refine our prompting makes it more likely that we will get the output we are hoping for.

QUESTIONS FOR REFLECTION AND DISCUSSION

1. What kinds of experiences have you had with AI prompting? Do you have an example of a prompt that worked exceptionally well? Maybe an example of a prompt gone wrong?

2. Check your imagination: in light of what we've learned about data processing, neural networks, machine learning, probability calculations, and large language models, why does the output generated by an AI chatbot depend so heavily on our inputs?

PART V

AI and the Work of Teaching and Learning

18

Becoming, Not Arriving
Committing to Playful Practice

WHETHER YOU'VE BEEN TEACHING for years, or if you are still very new to the teaching profession, I suspect you're on some kind of growth trajectory. Most teachers I've talked with would agree that they are better today than they were on their first day of teaching—teaching is the sort of work that gets better the more you practice it, after all. And I truly don't think any teacher sets out at the beginning of their career saying, "I'm going to be the most mediocre teacher I can be!" We all have something in us that wants to keep growing, keep improving, keep honing our craft, right?

This too is an exercise in imagination: I believe that growing as a teacher is a process of becoming, and this process of development is the sort of thing that continues to unfold throughout our careers. We never really "arrive" as teachers, but we can keep getting better if we commit to reflection, practice, and ongoing learning. I think this is particularly true for Christian educators: developing our capacity to teach "Christianly" is an opportunity for us to live out calling to faithfully follow Jesus.[1] Jesus' own words

---

1. I am always cautious about carelessly throwing around the language of "calling" with educators, because I think this can be used and abused to put

in the Gospel of Matthew give us a place to begin, as he says, "Whoever wants to be my disciple must deny themselves, take up their cross and follow me."[2] This is the heart of our calling as Christian educators!

But where do we go from there? I believe we all have some picture in our head of how our faith impacts our work as teachers—this is what I mean by teaching "Christianly." Some Christian teachers focus on the devotional aspects, others focus on providing a Christian perspective on the curriculum, still others on evangelizing students, and others on modeling Christian behavior. All of these are ways of expressing teaching Christianly, and I celebrate each of them! But even more foundationally, I challenge all Christian educators to think about their work of teaching Christianly as *working out our discipleship*, learning to more enthusiastically follow Jesus day-by-day through our work as educators.[3] And I want to suggest that we can approach this through what I will call a commitment to playful practice.

This idea of "playful practice" connects strongly to creativity, and I want to encourage you as we start making an application to teaching and learning with AI to approach this as innately creative work. When I talk with educators about creativity, a common response I hear is along the lines of, "Ahh, I'm just not that creative . . ." I think this is because we often equate "creativity" with "being artistic." I'd like to encourage you to reframe creativity as being resourceful, generative, and flexible instead of "artistic," necessarily. Because resourcefulness, generativity, and flexibility are the sort of

unrealistic expectations on teachers. And perhaps Christian educators especially may fall prey to this kind of thinking because we are so eager to serve! But that said, I truly do believe that teaching Christianly is an occasion to live out our calling. I believe the calling of every believer—teacher or not—is most broadly stated as learning to more faithfully follow Jesus!

2. Matt 16:24.

3. I wrote a book on this topic; the title is *Always Becoming, Never Arriving: Developing an Imagination for Teaching Christianly*. The key idea is that growing as a Christian educator is all about discipleship, and we must commit to faithfully following Jesus even in the small things. I believe Jesus cares about how we arrange the desks in our classrooms, as this illustrates what we believe about how we are proclaiming "Jesus is Lord!," even in those small decisions.

things that we can certainly develop through playful practice! Let me say just a few more words about this before we wrap up this chapter.

Let's first talk about practice. The old saying is "practice makes perfect," but I think a more honest and realistic take is that "practice makes *permanent*." In his book *You Are What You Love*, James K. A. Smith talks a lot about the nature of habits and how developing habits actually helps us develop our loves—and helps us love the right things.[4] If you want to get better at playing the guitar, you simply must practice. If you want to get better at left-handed layups out on the basketball court, practicing is the only sure way to develop this skill. And, if you want to become a better teacher, learning more about promising teaching strategies *and putting them into practice* is probably the best way to get better. Likewise, teaching Christianly takes practice—being intentional, persevering, and (of course!) relying on the Holy Spirit's work in our lives are keys to maturing in our faith. We get better at the things we practice, and they become more habitual for us the more we practice.

Now let's talk about play. I've been leaning on the idea of imagination throughout this book, and I hope you are perceiving by now that I think that this kind of playful, imaginative work is quite central to our work as educators. More than that, I think play is helpful for us in learning to apply the big story to our work as educators. My friend and colleague Justin Bailey thinks a lot about imagination and play in relation to his field, theology. In his book *Interpreting Your World*, Bailey spends substantial time explaining how imaginative play can help us develop an aesthetic lens for understanding cultural development but then gets down to the basics of play, suggesting that "robust imaginative play" is in fact a key indicator of our ability to thrive as human beings.[5] Imaginative

---

4. While not a book about education explicitly, I have found *You Are What You Love* an exceptionally helpful book for guiding my own reflection on practice and habit-forming behaviors—in the positive sense. I recommend it to you for further encouragement as you think about this.

5. This idea comes from pp. 115–16 of Bailey, *Interpreting Your World*. This whole section is lovely, as it moves from very high-minded exploration of the

generativity is really what play is about—the capability we have as image-bearers of our Creator to joyfully and playfully develop the Creation by creating things ourselves.

My intent is that the rest of this book will be an investigation of this kind of "playful practice" approach toward AI in education through the lens of teaching Christianly. This will mean using the Christian imagination we discussed earlier—the contours of the big story—as the habit-forming guidance we need, even as we take a playful, generative approach to applying what we have learned about how AI works. This is a process of "becoming" and perhaps not "arriving," but we can definitely develop our knowledge and skills by playfully practicing implementing a Christian imagination for AI in education.

So how about it? Will you commit to playful practice?

KEY IDEA FROM THIS CHAPTER

"Playful practice" is a way for us to develop our capacities for teaching Christianly in many different aspects of our development as Christian educators, and we will apply this approach to considering how we might use AI for teaching and learning.

QUESTIONS FOR REFLECTION AND DISCUSSION

1. Have you heard the phrase "teaching Christianly" before? What connections do you make to this concept as it was explained in this chapter?

2. What do you make of the idea of creativity as "robust imaginative play" that can encompass resourcefulness, generativity, and flexibility? Does this help you reframe creativity as something within your reach? Why or why not?

---

role of play in creating great works of art and ends up talking about how his own kids make up games and how seeing play through the eyes of children can help boost our own "imaginative generativity."

19

Teaching and Learning
Two Different (but Related) Activities

A COLLEAGUE ONCE ASKED me for my take on the difference between teaching and learning, and in response I quipped, "If the students aren't learning, can you say you're really teaching?" I'm not proud of myself for this, but I know there have been times that I "taught" a lesson but my students didn't really learn very much. When that happens, I believe I have a professional responsibility to rethink it and reteach it. My role as a teacher is to ensure my students learn—this is, in fact, the whole point of the work of teaching!

Teaching and learning are obviously related activities, but there are clear differences in the work of teachers and students. Students do the hard work of moving from not knowing to knowing, from having rudimentary understanding to having deep and comprehensive understanding, from not yet having the skills to being skillful. And teachers' work is guiding students into this knowledge, understanding, and skill, by carefully crafting instruction, implementing those plans, and assessing their students' learning.

Part V: AI and the Work of Teaching and Learning

I think it might be helpful for us to think about the different work being done by students and teachers as being the result of the different offices they hold. You might first think of an "office" as a place—the doctor's office, an accountant's office, a pastor's office, and—especially in school—the principal's office. But what if we think of that physical space as the place where a kind of authority is wielded by a person who has a particular role. The doctor's office is the place where she works the authority of her role as a medical professional. Likewise, the accountant's office, the pastor's office, and—yes—the principal's office too: the office is the place where they practice the responsibilities that come with their authority.

But let's rethink the "office" as being the role rather than the place. As a teacher, you have "official" duties—rights and responsibilities—that come with your role. And as an "official," maybe it makes sense to think about the "office of the teacher" as being related to the authority we hold because of that role. And, for Christian teachers in particular, a consciousness of our office is essentially important. We view ourselves as being called by God himself into the office of teacher! And teaching Christianly means keeping our office—and the associated authority we bear—in mind through a sense of office consciousness.[1] Because of your role, your office, you have particular rights and responsibilities.

But let's also imagine the "office of the student"—a student might also be an office-bearer in this light, with rights and responsibilities of their own. They should be able to expect to be treated with dignity and respect, to have teachers who show up ready to teach, to be held to high standards for their own work, and to be expected to *learn*.

---

1. In his book *The Craft of Christian Teaching*, John Van Dyk reminds us, "As a Christian teacher you need to develop a sense of *office consciousness*. Such office consciousness guarantees that you will not reduce teaching to a humdrum menial task, a routine for which you receive a monthly paycheck. Office consciousness will help you to connect your work to the calling of God, and therefore, to the work of God himself. Office consciousness equips you to see that every morning anew you enter the classroom as a place where the Kingdom of God must come to expression. Office consciousness reminds you that together with others you must strive to do his will" (p. 41).

Teaching and Learning

Central to the office of the teacher is the work of teaching. Central to the office of the student is the work of learning. These are related tasks but not the same. And likewise, the roles—the offices—of the teacher and the student are different, with different rights and responsibilities.

How might this kind of office-conscious approach impact our work? Well, on the one hand, I practice what I call the Golden Rule for Teachers, which is "never ask students to do something you are unwilling to do yourself." On the other hand, I try to not expect students to already have the knowledge, understanding, and skills that we have developed over a long time. The work they are doing is about learning. The work that I am doing is about ensuring that they learn. The different offices we hold means that we do different work from each other. And if the work we are doing is different, I believe this also means that we should have different expectations for the way teachers and students do their work, the tools they use, the structures we put in place, and perhaps even the policies we might use to guide the way work is done.

Here's the clincher: when it comes to technology for teaching and learning, we shouldn't expect students to use it in the same ways that teachers do. This reflects the difference in the offices they hold and the quality of the work they each are doing as they teach and learn.

KEY IDEA FROM THIS CHAPTER

The work of teaching and the work of learning are not the same, and likewise, the work of teachers and the work of learners each take on a unique character. This means that there will likely be substantial differences between teacher uses and student uses of technology.

Part V: AI and the Work of Teaching and Learning

QUESTIONS FOR REFLECTION AND DISCUSSION

1. The idea that teachers and students have an "office"—an "official" role with distinct rights and responsibilities—might be a new one for you. Does this help you imagine the work of teaching and learning in a different way than you have considered it before? Why or why not?

2. What do you make of the suggestion that teachers and students should use technology in different ways because of the different roles they play in the classroom? To what degree to you agree, and how would you argue with that idea?

20

Rosie the Robot
Ensuring Humans Do the Right Work

When our family bought a new home several years ago, we received a gift from the bank when we closed on our mortgage: a Roomba. If you are not familiar, a Roomba is a robot vacuum cleaner that uses sensors to navigate and clean floors. It detects obstacles, dirt, and edges and then moves in patterns to cover the area to be cleaned. Brushes and suction collect debris into a bin, and then the robot returns to its charging station until the next time a vacuuming is needed.

I have to confess, I was pretty excited to bring this device home and get it set up in the new house. This was part of my imagination for living in "the future" that was promised by the Jetsons. The Jetsons are a cartoon family who live in a futuristic world of the 2060s (the cartoon originally debuted in the 1960s) and have all kinds of amazing technological innovations in their lives, from video phone calls, to voice-operated computers, to flying cars, to machines that brush your teeth for you. So, while they accurately predicted some things (video calls and voice-operated smart devices have become normal), they were off the mark—so far, at

Part V: AI and the Work of Teaching and Learning

least—for some things. (Because I don't think I want an automatic tooth-brushing machine!)

But from my watching *Jetsons* reruns in my childhood, there was one innovation I always wanted: Rosie the Robot, the Jetsons' robotic maid. Rosie the Robot cooked meals, did the dishes, and vacuumed the house for the Jetsons. And I wanted a robot maid who would do my chores for me, too. So perhaps you can imagine my excitement in bringing the Roomba home: here was part of my vision for a robot maid who would take care of things for me!

But here's the thing: the Roomba didn't really work out the way I hoped. Our couch is *just* the wrong height, so the Roomba would sometimes get stuck under the edge of the couch and run and run until its battery was dead. Because of the layout of our kitchen and dining room, there were a few corners and crannies where the robot just couldn't quite get all the dust and crumbs. One time, the door to the basement steps got left open, and we found the Roomba upside-down, halfway down the stairs.

My dreams of a robot maid did not translate into reality, and the Roomba has ended up back in the box, in the basement storage room.

Andy Crouch has a term for this sort of thing: "boring robots." Crouch says, "Robots, it turns out, are amazing—but only before they arrive."[1] What he means is that the robots in our imagination are more wonderful than the reality once they are in our lives. This seems to be true for me when I think about generative AI as well. The first few times I use a new generative AI tool, I always feel a little wowed by the "magic" of the machine. But that magic is often short-lived, and I wind up feeling a little underwhelmed. That is not to say that the AI tools are not helpful in their way—they certainly can be! But I wonder, along with Crouch, if the potential of

---

1. This quote comes from p. 91 of Crouch's wonderful book, *The Life We're Looking For*. This is part of a chapter that is all about this idea of "boring robots." He explains how technology—including robots—often wind up letting us down because the promise is often hype and the reality doesn't carry through. He even uses ChatGPT as an example of the reality of the "boring robot" phenomenon.

generative AI might end up being more of a "boring robots" sort of thing?

I really want Rosie the Robot to clean my room. Instead, I have ChatGPT, which can't clean my room and instead seems to be changing the way my students think about writing in ways that seem negative. Perhaps you can relate? I want to avoid some work, but I'm trying to avoid particular kinds of work—and I think my students are as well.

But here's the thing: I believe that human beings are actually created to work. Work is not a bad thing, something to dodge or escape. In fact, God gave Adam work to do before the Fall! Genesis 2:15 states this plainly: "The Lord God took the man and put him in the garden of Eden to work it and take care of it."[2] Work is not evil; work is a *good* part of how God created us to be as humans. Because of the effects of the Fall, we might want to avoid work, and there are certainly aspects of work that might be unpleasant.

Let's stretch our imaginations here a bit: we can see ways in which work is impacted by the Fall, surely. But we can also see ways that we human beings—image-bearers of the Creator—can use our God-given creativity to innovate ingenious instruments that might make the work easier. This is also part of God's good design for humans: we can use the creative potential in Creation to craft beautiful things, and this might be part of how we are working towards the Restoration of all things.

The challenge, in our broken-but-beautiful, technology-rich world is discerning how to ensure humans are doing the *right* work!

KEY IDEA FROM THIS CHAPTER

The promise of machines making work easier is appealing and a common theme in human existence. But humans are also created to work—it is part of God's good design for us as human beings!

---

2. Gen 2:15.

Part V: AI and the Work of Teaching and Learning

QUESTIONS FOR REFLECTION AND DISCUSSION

1. Do you have an imagination for using tools—like Rosie the Robot, perhaps?—to make work easier? What informs your imagination about the concept of "work"?

2. This chapter closed with an implication that there is some work that is the "right" work for humans to do. What might that include for teachers? For students?

21

Doing the Right Work
Wisdom from Grandpa Mulder

MY GRANDPA MULDER WAS an amazing man. My grandparents had twelve children, and while they never had much money, their family was rich in so many other ways. Grandpa Mulder served as the custodian for the Christian high school I eventually attended, and everyone loved him. In the 1980s I had a front-row seat for seeing why he was so beloved, beginning when I was in the third grade: I got to spend a lot of one-on-one time with Grandpa, helping out with cleaning the school. While he would run the dust mop to sweep the floors, I emptied trash cans, cleared shavings out of pencil sharpeners, beat chalk dust out of erasers, and got to learn Grandpa's wisdom firsthand. I learned how to see dirt. I learned the importance of doing the job well the first time. And I learned that jobs that don't seem very glamorous are often, in fact, some of the most important work that happens in an organization.

Grandpa Mulder had a particular way of living out his calling, even in the less-than-remarkable aspects of cleaning and maintaining a school. He viewed his work as a good gift from God, and he embodied the fruit of the Spirit authentically and obviously. And while he took the work seriously, he also could be playful. For example, when he saw some kids riding their skateboards around the school grounds after the final bell rang, he thought, "That's a great idea!" And he got a skateboard of his own—and would regularly zip around campus managing a large trash can efficiently in each of his huge hands. He took his work seriously, but he was able to be playful as well. And thus, one of his famous catchphrases: "work is fun!"

Grandpa Mulder embodied "work is fun." He instilled it in his kids, and even in us grandkids, when we worked alongside him. I have carried "work is fun" with me into my own professional life. My own catchphrase is, "We GET to do this!"—an outgrowth of Grandpa's philosophy that work *is* fun. I fully understand that not every part of our work will always be enjoyable, but truly, I do enjoy the challenges. And, as I've already noted, I try to take a playful, imaginative approach to my work, and I'm encouraging you to do the same.

But perhaps "fun" isn't the word we would use in every situation as educators? Maybe, on some days, it's more honest to say, "the work is meaningful," or "the work is demanding but satisfying," or even "the work is difficult, and I'm feeling drained today." Even on the hard days of teaching, I hope that we can all find joy in the opportunities we have to speak into the lives of our students, because the work of education is about *formation* and not just *information*.[1] The incredible opportunity we have as Christian educators is to influence not just what our students know but even how they will *be* in this world. What an incredible privilege!

---

1. I borrowed this concept from James K. A. Smith, who describes education as a way of shaping what we love, not just what we think. I particularly love this section from the introduction to his book *Desiring the Kingdom*: "What if education . . . is not primarily about the absorption of ideas and information, but about the formation of hearts and desires? What if we began by appreciating how education not only gets into our head but also (and more fundamentally) grabs us by the gut? What if education was primarily concerned with shaping our hopes and passions—our visions of 'the good life'—and not merely about the dissemination of data and information as inputs to our thinking? What if the primary work of education was the transforming of our imagination rather than the saturation of our intellect? . . . What if education wasn't first and foremost about what we know, but about what we love?" (pp. 17–18).

Doing the Right Work

This idea of doing meaningful, demanding, satisfying, hard work—and maybe even being able to find it "fun"—might seem countercultural, and not just in the realm of teaching. Work, as we noted in the last chapter, often feels like something people want to avoid or make less painful. But this might just be revealing a weakness of our imagination about the *goodness* of hard work.

Let me use an imaginative example to illustrate. I have enjoyed the *Harry Potter* series as a work of fantasy. The books tell a compelling story of good vs. evil, set in a magical world. Harry is a student learning to do magic—and finds magical solutions helpful in so many parts of his life. But at one point in the story, Harry refuses to use magic to do a very challenging task. A beloved character in the story is killed, and Harry decides to dig a grave by hand to honor the memory and sacrifice of his friend. He could have used magic to do this work very quickly, but the rapidity of that would not be as meaningful, and doing it "the hard way"—even with the blisters and sweat—was in fact the *better* way. This is, I think, an example of goodness of hard work. It was right, meaningful, and ultimately more satisfying *because* it was hard.[2]

Now that might be a silly, fictional illustration, but I hope you see the point I am making: hard work is, in fact, a good thing! Work is not something to be avoided. Teaching is hard work, but it is *good* work. Learning is hard work, but it is *good* work.

It's possible to use technology in "magical" ways that might seem like they are helping us avoid working hard. But I believe there is a cost to this: we give ourselves the opportunity to do work that actually matters. This is not to say we shouldn't use tools to help us do the meaningful, important, hard work. Even in my example of Harry digging the grave without magic, he used a shovel to do the digging.

The point is this: if we are trying to avoid work, we might be missing the point. Work is part of God's good design for Creation,

---

2. The recounting of this important scene is in chapter 24 of *Harry Potter and the Deathly Hallows*, where we see how the digging of the grave is part of how Harry seeks to both deal with his own deep grief and anger, as well as honor his friend's memory. Rowling, *Harry Potter and the Deathly Hallows*, 477–81.

part of how God created humans to be, and we can find meaning and satisfaction in hard work. The teacher in the book of Ecclesiastes reminds us of this: "I know that there is nothing better for people than to be happy and to do good while they live. That each of them may eat and drink, and find satisfaction in all their toil—this is the gift of God."[3] The challenge is ensuring that we do the right work and use the right tools to do that work.

Perhaps then we might—like Grandpa Mulder skateboarding his way across campus—discern the truth that "work is fun."

KEY IDEA FROM THIS CHAPTER

Work is part of God's good design for human beings, and we can—and should—find meaning and satisfaction in good, hard work.

QUESTIONS FOR REFLECTION AND DISCUSSION

1. What did you first think of when you heard the phrase "work is fun"? What might that reveal about your imagination for what work is all about?
2. Make an AI connection: how can we use AI as a tool (perhaps like a shovel?) in a way that honors doing important, meaningful, satisfyingly good work?

---

3. Eccl 3:12–13.

22

Ethical Implementation
Where the Christian Imagination Rubber Hits the Road

IN THE FALL OF 2024 I attended a large, secular conference in my field of educational technology. I've attended this conference many times in the past, and it is a great way to keep a finger on the pulse of where things are in the world of research regarding EdTech and how it is being implemented. What amazed me in 2024 was the fact that at least *half* of the sessions at this conference had titles that included terms like artificial intelligence, machine learning, or large language models. A great many of these sessions were research-oriented presentations of ways educators at all levels were using artificial intelligence as part of their processes for teaching and learning. Generative AI is in the zeitgeist, and everyone—even researchers at major universities—is somewhere on the spectrum of enthusiastic to concerned about how it is being implemented in educational settings.

I attended many presentations related to AI over the days of the conference, and it was interesting to note how many of those sessions included the phrase "ethical implementation." Everyone seems to be interested in using AI ethically. And I'm truly glad to hear that, because I think it would be very easy to use AI in very *unethical* ways as well!

This topic of "ethical implementation" came up in conversation with a friend over a cup of coffee, between sessions at the conference. He raised an intriguing question: "Everyone keeps using those words: 'ethical implementation.' But do you think they all mean the same thing when they say that?" We joked that we should do some research on these EdTech researchers and survey them to find out their thinking: "What determines what is 'ethical' when it comes to AI?" I suspect, given the diverse nature of the attendees at that particular conference, that there would be a wide variety of responses to this question.

But this also has me thinking and wondering if there are some ways that Christians might agree together on what "ethical implementation" might look like in real life. I think the big story we've been reflecting on together throughout these pages might help us to get a better, healthier imagination for ethical implementation of AI in practice.

Considering Creation, let's remember that God does not make junk, and because human beings are created in his image, we too have incredible creative capacities. When it comes to our work as teachers, we can create resources in innovative ways to great effect—developing materials, solving problems, and leveraging tools to craft delightful things. Part of ethical implementation of AI should be informed by this truth: we are beauty-creators, and we should work to create beautiful things.

Considering the Fall, let's remember that human beings are broken, and the things we devise and develop and do are likewise twisted by sin. When it comes to our work as teachers, we must recall that we will not be able to do the work perfectly, and there are times we are going to get it wrong. Part of ethical implementation of AI, then, should be a careful reckoning of the potential ways that the tools could be used to harm others, even unintentionally.

Considering Redemption, let's remember that Christ has done the redeeming work to buy back all that was damaged by the Fall. Scars remain, but Jesus' salvage operation makes it possible

Ethical Implementation

for us to again be in right relationship with God and our neighbors. When it comes to our work as teachers, let's keep this idea at the forefront: the way we use technologies and tools should point towards this right relationship nature—loving, caring, compassionate, self-controlled. Part of ethical implementation, then, should be celebrating our restored nature, emphasizing this being made right with God.

Considering Restoration, let's remember that God is at work, making all things new. And while he certainly does not *need* us (he's God and is completely powerful to do things without any human intervention!), he delights in us and *invites* us to work our small, human ways towards the Restoration of all things. When it comes to our work as teachers, this means we have a very real opportunity to work to bridge the gap between the brokenness we see still existing in the world around us and ways that we can discern God's good design in Creation. Part of ethical implementation of AI should be using it in ways that are restorative, demonstrating the nature of "new creation" life.

Okay, that might still feel pretty philosophical, so let me give five practical principles that I believe are in harmony with the contours of the big story. I think these principles can give us guidance for ethical implementation of generative AI in educational settings.

- First, let's consider *privacy*. Keeping personal information private is a key idea here! This would mean, for example, avoiding uploading student information into an AI interface and resisting the temptation to give these powerful tech companies more data than they ought to have. Every prompt we enter into the AI adds to the database, and keeping confidential things private is a key part of ethical usage.

- Second, let's emphasize *relationships*. We can use AI to do lots of things, but let's consider the person on the other end of the usage. For example, if I am using AI to write a letter to my grandma, how would she feel knowing that the AI was really the one to write the letter? Let's prioritize humanity in our fellow human beings and commit to using AI in ways that make us *more* humane.

- Third, let's think about the nature of *integrity*. Integrity is about being who you say you are and being a whole, real human being. Let's not outsource our thinking to the machines! Maybe it helps to think of it this way: while it might be tempting to use AI as your "auto-pilot," a healthier approach is to treat AI as your "co-pilot," with you still in control and not giving the AI too much power. (It is a machine, after all.) A mantra I have tried to instill in my students is "first draft, worst draft." What I mean by this is that we can, and should, expect to keep working at things, to keep learning, to keep developing ideas and practices. As a practical step, I like the 80 percent rule: "The AI can get you 80 percent of the way there, but it will never get you 100 percent of the way there."[1] We should *expect* the need to revise the things generated by the AI. An ethical approach would be to never expect the AI to do all the work for us.

- Fourth, let's practice *transparency*. What I mean by transparency is being up front about when and how we are using AI. If we feel like we need to make excuses for the situations in which we are using AI, that is probably not going to be an ethical way to use the AI as part of our work. We should be perfectly comfortable telling colleagues, administrators, parents, and even our students about the ways we are using AI in our work.

- Finally, let's consider the role of *humility*. We must be able to admit that this is a brave new world and that we are truly still learning how to use AI. This implies, unfortunately, that we are going to get it wrong sometimes, and we must be humble enough to confess when we get it wrong, apologize, and work to make things right.

---

1. I encountered this idea in the terms of service for MagicSchool, a company that produces an AI toolkit for educators, including the "80–20 approach." Magic School, "Terms of Service."

Ethical Implementation

These kinds of principles can help to guide us in the ways we will practically use AI as part of our teaching toolbox and even for our students' potential use of AI for their work of learning. And the good news for us as we stumble along in learning how to use AI as part of education: the big story of Scripture can illuminate a pathway for us actually do this work!

KEY IDEA FROM THIS CHAPTER

Many people talk about "ethical implementation" of artificial intelligence, and the big story of Scripture can help us to truly be ethical in our approach to using AI in education.

QUESTIONS FOR REFLECTION AND DISCUSSION

1. Check your imagination: how does the big story of Scripture illustrate ethical usage of AI in education?
2. As you consider the five principles for ethical implementation at the end of this chapter, what was a new idea for you? How can these principles help you ensure ethical AI usage?

23

AI and Discipleship
Avoiding an Educational Technology Arms Race

TAKE A MOMENT TO think, and jot down an answer to this question: *Why did you become an educator?*

I think some of us would answer that question "because I love kids!" And certainly, if you *don't* love kids, this profession is probably not for you![1] The opportunity we get to speak into kids' lives is one we should certainly not take lightly.

I think some of us would answer that question "because I love _____!" (Fill in the blank with your favorite subject.) Some of us *love* history, or music, or geometry, or physics, and we want our students to love that content too!

I think some of us would answer that question "because I love *teaching!*" The work of teaching: it's the best—and perhaps most demanding—work on the face of this planet. Seeing the spark in

---

1. In my book *Always Becoming, Never Arriving*, I describe loving kids as the "barrier to entry" for the teaching profession. Most of us have, unfortunately, had a teacher along the way that we are pretty sure didn't love kids. What a terrible situation that is—for teacher and students alike! Chapter seven of the book is all about loving the kids we teach and the joyful opportunities we have to foster their development and growth.

AI and Discipleship

a student's eye when they first understand something is one of the best feelings, isn't it? The joyful challenge of helping someone move from "novice" to "knower" is incredibly gratifying.

We all have some reason that we joined this profession. But, when I'm completely honest about it, I find that it can be difficult sometimes to keep that reason in mind. Things don't always work out the way that I wish they would. Those kids I love so much can also behave like entirely alien creatures. That subject I love so well isn't always loved as much by others, sapping my enthusiasm. And this arcane art of planning and enacting instructional strategies—not to mention the most mystical part of all, assessing students' knowledge, understanding, and skills—can begin to feel like more of a burden than a blessing. On the hardest days, we might truly find ourselves asking, "Why did I become a teacher again??"

I think that there are many reasons for this, but technology is probably on the list of challenges for many of us who serve as educators. The magnetic pull of screens is hard competition for even the most engaging teachers. And this can begin to feel like a real battle. Does the glow of a student's Chromebook pull their attention away from what should be their object of focus? Does the student's smartphone, with every social network known to humanity at their fingertips, seem far more engaging than anything you have to offer? Perhaps it's no wonder we might want to fight fire with fire—trying to use new and novel technologies to capture students' attention and engagement? To combat their apathy, distraction, and disengagement with something novel?[2]

I wonder if this is the case with generative AI in education today. Are we intent on using this flashy new tool/toy as a way of trying to win the war on attention?

My concern with this is that I think it only adds to the potential educational technology arms race between teachers and students.

---

2. In her book *The War on Learning*, Elizabeth Losh describes the way teachers and students line up, with different technological weapons in their respective arsenals. While the book was written in 2014 and some of the technologies she describes have shifted in the intervening years, I think that the picture she paints is still a reality for many teachers' experiences, in both K-12 and higher education.

Part V: AI and the Work of Teaching and Learning

I can imagine a situation where teachers use AI to create what they hope will be engaging assignments. The students will then use AI to help them complete the assignments—or even outsource their thinking to the AI. And then the teachers, demoralized and overwhelmed, might use AI to help them grade the work—or even outsource their feedbacking to the machines. We worry about students cheating with AI, so we begin to use AI-powered tools to check whether students are using AI to cheat. This feels like a race to the bottom, where human beings simply become mediators between AI-powered agents! I don't like the implication of that at all—and I don't think it's in line with a Christ-centered vision of teaching and learning.

Let's come back to the imagining we've been doing together as we think about AI. I think that we certainly can use AI in ways that are resonant with the big story and ways that are working towards Restoration. But to do this, we need to use AI tools ethically and responsibly, and we need to teach our students to use these powerful tools ethically and responsibly as well.

Along those lines, let me offer four words of encouragement.

First, AI is not always going to be the right approach—or, more broadly speaking, digital tools are not always going to be the right approach. I urge teachers to think carefully about choosing the right tools to support their teaching and their students' learning. Sometimes pencil and paper is the right tool. Sometimes an Internet-connected Chromebook is the right tool. Sometimes a tub of Play-Doh is the right tool. Sometimes an AI chatbot is the right tool. We need to carefully consider when and how we leverage digital technologies in light of students' needs, the needs of the curriculum, and even our own teaching styles. AI has a lot of potential, but we need to use it discerningly.

Second, I want to encourage us to keep in mind that human beings are created in God's image, and this fact must impact the way we think about using AI as part of teaching and learning. God is the Creator. We, as his image-bearers, are created to create! AIs, for all their power, do not *create*—they *construct*. Remember that AIs are playing a word-association game, predicting what the user

AI and Discipleship

is hoping to see rather than truly creating a novel idea. We—and our students—need to understand the difference between constructing and creativity. When we use AI as part of the teaching and learning process, we should emphasize human creativity and not expect or even *allow* the AI to disrupt this important aspect of what it means to be human! AI should *support* humans doing human work rather than *replace* human work.

Thirdly, we—and our students—need to understand that AI is a powerful *tool*, and we can certainly use tools to support teaching and learning. Picking up on the idea that humans are created to create, we can recognize that we use all sorts of tools for all sorts of work. This is, in fact, part of how we live out our creativity as image-bearers. That said, students need instruction in how to use tools. In the same way that we would carefully instruct students using other powerful tools (imagine your students using power saws or nail guns), we need to *teach* and *supervise* the use of AI.

Finally, let's come back to the reason you wanted to become a teacher. Whether it's because you love kids, love content, or love the work of teaching—or all of these together!—the heart of teaching Christianly is discipleship. I think working with AI is a great opportunity for us to put skin on this work of discipleship. We are rightly concerned about cheating. (But we should also remember that cheating didn't come into existence with ChatGPT!) Students may need discipline if they are misusing powerful tools. But more than that, they need *discipling* about what it means to be human, about the joy of doing hard work, about living out their calling to faithfully follow Jesus!

KEY IDEA FROM THIS CHAPTER

We must be mindful about the right role of educational technologies and how both we and our students are using them. We have an opportunity and responsibility to disciple young people, including in the way they think about and use AI.

Part V: AI and the Work of Teaching and Learning

QUESTIONS FOR REFLECTION AND DISCUSSION

1. What do you make of the idea of educational technology as an "arms race" between teachers and students? Does that metaphor resonate with you? What other metaphors would you use to describe the relationship between teachers, students, and technology?

2. What kinds of practical steps could Christian teachers take to disciple students in using AI in ways that promote Restoration?

24

Being Brave
Learning from Orville Wright

EARLY IN MY CAREER in higher education, a colleague recommended that I read Gordon MacKenzie's fabulous book *Orbiting the Giant Hairball*.[1] MacKenzie was a long-time leader at Hallmark, the company most famous for their greeting cards. The book is part-memoir, part-advice manual for rising leaders, and all about creativity and being gracious to yourself as you are learning.

My favorite chapter in the book is entitled "Orville Wright." It is a very short chapter. It's so short, the whole chapter is just one sentence long. Here's the chapter:

> "Orville Wright did not have a pilot's license."[2]

---

1. Isn't that a wild title? The basic idea: large organizations often start to take on the tangled and convoluted shape of a giant hairball—something easy to get tied up in and ensnared. We might want to go flying off on our own, but that's not how organizational life works! So, MacKenzie recommends *orbiting* the giant hairball: not getting tangled up in organizational bureaucracy but also not going it alone, instead using the "gravity" of the organization to propel your own creativity and innovation. It's a great read for folks interested in a little creative inspiration.

2. MacKenzie, *Orbiting the Giant Hairball*, 191. The facing page has a wonderful photograph of the Wright Brothers' plane, a good reminder of just how

Part V: AI and the Work of Teaching and Learning

This is a good reminder when you are engaging something new. It's not that training and preparation aren't important and necessary. The Wright Brothers certainly had mechanical know-how and had spent substantial time creating that first powered airplane. They were as prepared as they could have been for that initial test flight.

But, at some point, Orville simply had to strap into the pilot's seat and give it a go.

Do you wonder if he was terrified? Thrilled? Some combination? The thing is, being brave doesn't mean you aren't scared. It means doing the thing *even when you are scared.*

I think it's worth remembering that we regularly ask students to undertake challenging, demanding things that they have never done before—things that are perhaps scary for them. I think that we adults probably forget that feeling—and just how brave we must be standing on the edge of something new. We can prepare and prepare, and at some point, we just have to strap in and give it a go. We expect our students to be brave enough to learn. We might have to practice being brave enough to learn ourselves as well!

This is my invitation to you, particularly if generative AI has you feeling a little nervous: tap into your inner Orville Wright and give it a whirl. In the next few chapters, we're going to explore a few use cases for AI and think through the possibilities and pitfalls in light of a biblically informed imagination, using the Creation-Fall-Redemption-Restoration motif to guide our thinking. My encouragement is to try it, so you can know from first-hand experience.

While there are a ton of AI-powered tools available today, I am going to focus on ChatGPT in the examples we'll consider in the AI use cases that follow in the next few chapters. At the time of this writing, ChatGPT seems to occupy a lot of the mind space for many people when they start thinking about generative AI. ChatGPT is easy to use, and there is a free, publicly available version that anyone can use. And because there are new tools being developed all the time, I think it will make sense for us to just focus on one for now. The use cases I'm suggesting should work with

---

terrifying that first flight must have been!

Being Brave

any generative AI chatbot you are able to access, and I encourage you to try things out firsthand. (If you're well on your way, already playing with AI tools by now, please be patient with those of us who are a little newer and perhaps still in the Orville Wright stage, okay?)

What will you do with your AI assistant? Here are ten just-for-fun prompts you might use as a beginning point for your exploration. Feel free to adapt the ideas here to your interests to help figure out what an AI can do! Head to https://chatgpt.com/ and enter some of these prompts in the text box on the page:

1. What are some fun things you can help me with?
2. Can you explain how you work in simple terms?
3. What's something surprising you can do that most people don't know about?
4. Can you help me make a simple meal plan for the week?
5. I'm planning a trip to New York City—what are some must-see places?
6. What are some fun and free activities to do with kids on a rainy day?
7. Can you help me write a friendly email to a colleague?
8. Can you write a short story about a dog who saves the day?
9. Explain photosynthesis to me like I'm in fifth grade.
10. Can you quiz me with five multiple-choice questions about Canada?

Particularly if you've never played around with an AI chatbot before, I hope you'll be willing to take a reasonable risk to try it out. Orville Wright did not have a pilot's license, and yet he was willing to take to the sky—and I hope you'll consider this permission to approach AI as playful practice that you *get* to do!

Part V: AI and the Work of Teaching and Learning

KEY IDEA FROM THIS CHAPTER

Sometimes the best way we can learn something is by diving right in and trying it firsthand.

QUESTIONS FOR REFLECTION AND DISCUSSION

1. What do you think of the idea of being brave enough to learn? Does this resonate with you as a teacher when you think about your own students? Does it resonate with you when you think about your own learning?

2. If you haven't yet, try out a few of the suggested prompts for ChatGPT in this chapter. What did you find out in the process of your exploration? What surprised you? What was confirmed for you?

PART VI

AI Use Cases

25

AI Use Case
Leveled Reading

THE BACKGROUND

Let's be candid: as much as we might wish that every student in a class can read at the same level, the truth is that students' reading abilities can vary wildly. A grade-seven class with twenty-five students might have an "average" reading level of grade seven. But this would probably mean there are some students who are reading at a high school level, some reading at a fifth-grade level, and maybe one or two at a second-grade reading level. Having a shared reading experience in this case could be very challenging—but what if we could start with a text "at grade level" and then adjust it so the content of the readings would be held constant, but the vocabulary and syntax of the reading could be varied to meet students where they are?

Part VI: AI Use Cases

PROMPTING GENERATIVE AI

Teachers can use an AI chatbot like ChatGPT to create leveled readings for their students. Here is an approach you might use.

Start by prompting the chatbot using the RAFT format to give some context for what you want it to generate. For example, consider the following prompt:

> I am a seventh-grade social studies teacher, and I need an article that I can use in my world geography class. I want an article that is about five hundred words in length that will help my students understand the physical and cultural geography of Central America and the Caribbean. I will use this as a background reading to give them a background in the key characteristics of this region. Write an explanation of the physical geography and unique cultural factors that make Central America and the Caribbean both similar to and different from surrounding regions. Use an expressive and engaging tone that conveys the importance of this topic in a way that will be relevant for middle school students.

The next thing you should do is take time to read through the resulting output that the chatbot generates—remember, you should only expect the AI to get you 80 percent of the way there. Make any edits you might need to for content or tone. Once you have a solid article for students to read, copy and be ready to paste it back into the chatbot.

A new prompt: "I'm going to give you a piece of text. Keep the content the same, but rewrite it at a fourth-grade reading level. Here is the text to rewrite: <paste in your revised article here>."

Again, be sure to check the result to see if it is correct in content and tone.

You can repeat the copy and paste with the same prompt, just changing the grade level: "Rewrite this at a econd-grade reading level" or "Rewrite this at a tenth-grade reading level." You can also use Lexile levels, if you are familiar with this way of describing reading levels—your prompt might look like "Rewrite this at Lexile 550." You may need to make a few more adjustments, but using

AI Use Case

this strategy will result a collection of readings on the same topic at different reading levels.

GUIDANCE FOR USING THIS STRATEGY

Keeping in mind the five principles for ethical implementation, consider the following:

- Privacy—Do not enter students' personal information into the chatbot. Be mindful of the way you might use copyrighted materials as well!
- Relationships—Adapt your prompting as needed, based on what you know of your students! Tailor the results you get by re-prompting as needed to get a result more closely aligned to your students' needs and interests.
- Integrity—Be mindful of the temptation to not take the time to edit and make modifications after the first result is generated. You wouldn't be excited if your students submitted the AI's output as their work without taking the time to rework it, would you?
- Transparency—Be prepared to share with your students, their parents, and your colleagues where these readings have come from.
- Humility—If you don't get the results you are hoping for, admit it! Hopefully if you use these first four principles to the full, you won't have to apologize for any unfortunate results.

We certainly always have to be mindful of using AI-powered tools in ways that affirm the "heart-soul-mind-strength complex designed for love" nature of what it means to be human. What do you think: is using AI to respond to the reading needs of your students a Restoration-oriented approach for leveraging the power of this tool?

Part VI: AI Use Cases

KEY IDEA FROM THIS CHAPTER

AI chatbots are well suited to generate leveled readings, which can be a real blessing for students. This can be a Restoration-oriented way to use AI as part of the teaching and learning endeavor.

QUESTIONS FOR REFLECTION AND DISCUSSION

1. Thinking through the big story, can you name ways that this approach for using AI could potentially illustrate both the goodness of Creation as well as the brokenness of the Fall? What should we keep thinking about if we would implement this approach in our own teaching?

2. Try using the prompting suggestions in this chapter, but apply them to your own content, grade level, and context. What kind of results did you get? If you didn't get the results you were hoping for, what else could you try for prompting the chatbot?

26

AI Use Case
Generating Review Questions and Scripts

THE BACKGROUND

Teachers' time is certainly precious, and we constantly make determinations about the best ways to spend our time. Using generative AI can be a potential time-saver, so we can prioritize relationship-driven parts of our work. Two examples of potentially time-intensive tasks that could be readily supported by generative AI are generating review questions and creating scripts.

There is substantial research that supports the use of frequent, low-stakes (that is, ungraded) quizzing of key material to help students master and retain the key ideas.[1] Depending on the curriculum resources you have available, you might have a substantial bank of potential questions you could use for this sort of regular review. But if not, an AI chatbot could be a great way to quickly and efficiently create a bank of questions that you could use.

---

1. James Lang's book *Small Teaching* is full of research-based strategies to support students' mastery of content. He has a whole chapter about the benefits of quizzing to foster long-term recall of learning.

Part VI: AI Use Cases

Many teachers in a variety of contexts use simple, creative dramatics as part of helping students engage the content, play around with ideas, develop presentation skills, and practice creative responses to their learning. Finding a good script that is closely aligned to the content can be a challenge, and writing your own scripts can take a lot of time. Instead, using an AI chatbot to generate the first draft could be a real time-saver.

PROMPTING GENERATIVE AI

Teachers can use an AI chatbot like ChatGPT to generate all sorts of instructional materials, including review questions and scripts. Here are a few prompts you might try using. Remember that you're likely to get better results by spending a little more time writing a clear prompt—I recommend using the RAFT format to give some more context for the sort of output you are hoping for. Here are a few sample prompts you might try using:

> "I am a high school biology teacher, and my students have recently been learning about the processes cells use for getting energy and raw materials and getting rid of waste products. I need a set of review questions for them to practice the vocabulary and recall the key ideas of these processes. Create a list of thirty multiple choice questions to help review these key concepts: photosynthesis, cellular respiration, ATP, mitochondria, chloroplasts, glucose, aerobic respiration, anerobic respiration, fermentation, diffusion, passive transport, active transport, endocytosis, exocytosis. Each multiple-choice question should have question stem that is longer than the answer choices, and there should be four answer choices for each question."

> "I am a third-grade teacher, and my students have been learning multiplication facts in their math class. I need a set of straightforward word problems that will help them practice their math facts. Generate a list of twenty multiplication word problems that include examples that are relevant for third-grade students."

AI Use Case

"I am a middle school literature teacher, and my grade-six students are studying folklore and fables. Create the script for a readers' theater based on the story of the elves and the shoemaker. It should include seven roles, including at least two narrators, the shoemaker, his wife, and some elves. In the script, clearly indicate each role so the students will be able to easily track their lines. Make the script about five hundred words in length."

"I am a high school geometry teacher, and my students are learning about how to prove theorems. Create the script of a humorous conversation between the Greek geometer Euclid and three of his students, who are learning theorems 1–5 from *The Elements*. In the script, make it clear that the students are learning, and even though they have lots of questions of their teacher, they are capable of solving challenging problems and writing thoughtful proofs. Have Euclid give them lots of encouragement and praise as they learn."

GUIDANCE FOR USING THIS STRATEGY

Keeping in mind the five principles for ethical implementation, consider the following:

- Privacy—Be mindful about the temptation to use copyrighted work. And of course don't upload students' personal information in a publicly available AI chatbot.
- Relationships—Think about your students and their interests and preferences. These can be included into the prompts to make the output something that will really connect with students, bringing them joy and delight when they "see themselves" in the materials.
- Integrity—You will likely need to review and revise the output before using with students. Particularly for review questions, check to make sure that the questions are accurate—that there

is a correct answer among the answer choices, for example, and that they don't all have "C" for the correct answer, etc.

- Transparency—Be prepared to share with your students, their parents, and your colleagues that you used AI to help create these materials. Also be clear about the ways you modified the output from the chatbot, because that is ethical use.

- Humility—You might not be satisfied with the first attempt: that is okay! Practicing your prompting will help you get a better result in the long run. If you do find that you're getting results that are unhelpful or inappropriate, be humble enough to keep practicing.

Creating instructional resources can be a time-intensive and laborious process, but using an AI chatbot to support the creation of these kinds of materials can be an efficient way to get a strong start that you can then edit to make them suitable for using with your students. While there are always temptations to outsource our thinking and generative capabilities to the machines, the efficiency of creating resources this way can provide more time for you to do the work that only a real human being can do—the relational work that is central to good teaching!

KEY IDEA FROM THIS CHAPTER

AI chatbots can help teachers create all kinds of materials to use with students, including review questions and scripts. Using AI to support you in generating these kinds of resources can allow more time for the relational work that only humans can do.

QUESTIONS FOR REFLECTION AND DISCUSSION

1. Thinking through the big story, can you name ways that this approach for using AI could potentially illustrate both the goodness of Creation as well as the brokenness of the Fall?

AI Use Case

What should we keep thinking about if we would implement this approach in our own teaching?

2. Try using the prompting suggestions in this chapter, but apply them to your own content, grade level, and context. What kind of results did you get? If you didn't get the results you were hoping for, what else could you try for prompting the chatbot?

27

AI Use Case
Rubric Development

THE BACKGROUND

A question I regularly get from teachers when working with them on AI-related tasks is "can the AI grade my students' work?" I understand that impulse completely. I have joked before that I teach for free, and they pay me to grade papers. (Joking, joking!) Doing good assessment of learning takes a ton of time, and it can be frustrating work—because we often see with immediacy and fine detail where our teaching may have fallen short of what students truly needed to master the content. I am sympathetic to teachers who want to have AI support for this work!

That said, I have grave concerns about outsourcing the important work of providing feedback on learning to the machines. I think it is possible to copy and paste a student's work into an AI chatbot and prompt it to critique the strengths and weaknesses of the student's work. Honestly, I've never tried this because it makes me feel pretty icky. I've heard educators complain about their students not doing their own work and giving over their thinking by

AI Use Case

having the AI do the work for them, short-circuiting their learning in the process. This approach to assessing students' work strikes me as being basically the same thing, just on the teacher's side of things. This feels like a double standard to me: to expect students to not use AI to avoid work they deem unpleasant but for teachers to do just that.

I do think, however, that it's totally appropriate to use generative AI tools to help with the developing assessment materials. Specifically, I think that AI can be an excellent way to devise rubrics. Writing a good rubric can be a time-intensive endeavor, but using AI to help with this work can free up time for the teacher to actually *use* that rubric to give students real feedback on their learning.

PROMPTING GENERATIVE AI

Creating a careful prompt makes all the difference for the actual rubric that is generated. Spending a few more minutes on the front end to be specific about what you need for the output can pay off for less reworking afterward. Here are a few ideas for how you might prompt the AI chatbot to generate a rubric.

First, you might think about simply uploading the whole prompt you would give to students for the project you are assigning, give the chatbot some further context (think RAFT), and see what kind of result you get—which you would, of course, have to manipulate a bit to make sure it is exactly what you need. Consider, for example, this prompt for a fifth-grade science class studying biomes. It's a lengthy prompt because getting a good result requires starting with a good explanation of what you want the chatbot to do. (Remember: garbage in, garbage out!)

> I am a fifth-grade teacher, and students in my science class are going to be researching different biomes (like desert, tropical rainforests, tundra, etc.). I need a rubric I can use to give them feedback on their work. Here is the project description that I will give to the students: create

a rubric based on the information in this description that will help me give them feedback on their work.

Project Overview

You and your team will become *biome experts*! Your job is to research one of Earth's major biomes and create a colorful, informative poster to teach others about it. You'll have three class periods (forty-five minutes each) to research, plan, and create your poster together. Use your time wisely and work as a team!

Your Task

Work in teams of three students to create a poster that teaches the rest of the class about your assigned biome.

What to Include on Your Poster

Your poster should be neat, colorful, and include the following:

1. The name of your biome—write it in *big, bold letters* at the top of the poster.
2. Pictures and Drawings—include at least four pictures or drawings that show what your biome looks like. These could be:
   - Animals that live there
   - Types of plants
   - The land or scenery
   - People living or working in that biome
3. Written Descriptions—write at least five to seven sentences (you can split this up across different sections) that explain:
   - What the weather and climate are like (hot, cold, dry, wet, seasons, etc.)
   - What types of plants and animals live there (and how they survive)
   - How humans live in this biome (homes, clothing, food, transportation)
   - Any other interesting facts about your biome!

Create the rubric using four levels of performance for each criteria, and use student-friendly language, so they will clearly understand what is meant by each level of performance.

Another approach you might consider for creating a rubric is not giving a more general description of the project but a very clear explanation of what you want the resulting rubric to look like. For example, consider this prompt:

> I am a high school English teacher, and after reading and discussing Shakespeare's *Romeo and Juliet*, we are going to watch a film adaptation. The students will write a literary analysis comparing and contrasting the play and the film, including characterization, dialogue and use of language, tone and mood, plot or character changes, portrayal of conflict, and audience impact. I need a rubric to help me give them feedback on their essays. The rubric should include the following criteria: Thesis and Focus, Use of Comparison Criteria, Evidence and Examples, Analysis and Interpretation, Organization and Structure, and Use of Conventions (Grammar, Spelling, and Punctuation). Create the rubric with three levels of proficiency for each criterion (Developing, Proficient, and Exemplary), and use teen-friendly language in the descriptors for each level of proficiency for each criterion.

There are many ways you could adapt these basic approaches to writing a rubric, so I would encourage you to explore, play, and iterate to get to the sort of rubric you are hoping for.

GUIDANCE FOR USING THIS STRATEGY

The big story of Scripture ought to inform the way we think about assessing our students' work. In our sinful, fallen state, we might view work as something to avoid. But it's important to remember the truth that work is part of the goodness of Creation—Adam had work to do even before the Fall! So, let's remember that while there are parts of the work that might seem unpleasant, we can look for redemptive, Restoration-oriented ways to do the work. Assessment truly is a way that we can encourage our students in a way that a machine simply cannot; providing careful feedback is an opportunity to build up our relationship an individual who is also created in the image of our Creator. Clear criteria that help understand the conditions for success can be a blessing for our students—and for us as we provide feedback to the learners under our care.

Rubrics are a great way to ensure more dependability in the results as we assess students' learning, as it keeps the criteria for success very clear and consistent—for both students as they develop the work, as well as for teachers as they assess the products. Using an AI chatbot to support your development of rubrics can be a real time-saver, allowing you more opportunities for the relationship-driven work of actually *giving* feedback on the work!

KEY IDEA FROM THIS CHAPTER

Assessment can be a quagmire, but creating a rubric with the support of an AI chatbot can make the work more efficient, giving the teacher more time to give students real feedback on their learning.

QUESTIONS FOR REFLECTION AND DISCUSSION

1. Considering the five principles for ethical implementation—privacy, relationships, integrity, transparency, and humility—what are some guidelines you will use to direct the use of AI to generate rubrics or other assessment supports?

2. Try using the prompting suggestions in this chapter, but apply them to your own content, grade level, and context. What kind of results did you get? If you didn't get the results you were hoping for, what else could you try for prompting the chatbot?

28

AI Use Case
Creating Graphics

THE BACKGROUND

Teachers often are on the hunt for graphics they can use for illustrations and decorations. A web search can sometimes result in graphics that will be suitable, but there are also situations in which creating a specific graphic for a particular situation would be more useful. Also, there are times that the images found online are copyrighted; while teachers have quite a bit of freedom under fair use guidelines to use copyrighted materials for educational purposes, there is an aspect of modeling for students that should also be considered. If we expect students to use copyrighted materials appropriately—including citing their sources—we ought to be modeling these appropriate uses ourselves!

In the past few years, AI image-generators have become more versatile and thus more useful. Human hands have proven elusively difficult to render.[1] But even this challenge has gotten better, with

---

1. This, by the way, is not just an AI problem! Whatever your level of personal artistry, I suspect hands give you trouble. Have you ever tried to draw

more recent developments and refinements to the protocols for the AIs generating the images. ChatGPT has a built-in image generator called Dall-E. If you prompt ChatGPT to create an image, it can do so. This is a processing-intensive task usually takes significantly longer than generating text, and for the free version of ChatGPT, there is a limit to how many images you can generate in a day, so you may need to take that into account if you are using Dall-E to create images. You might also consider looking into other AI tools specifically designed for creating images.

PROMPTING GENERATIVE AI

As we have seen in the past few use cases, a more specific prompt will almost always get you a better result. The RAFT strategy may again prove valuable for you, but you might also need to consider iterating after getting one image. The process can be a little fussy to get a result that is just what you are looking for. Making time for playful practice can improve your ability to prompt for just what you are looking for.

Here are a few examples of fairly specific prompts that a teacher might use.

> "I am a second-grade teacher, and I need some clip art images that I can use for my class newsletter. Please generate a collection of black-and-white clipart-style images of kids learning math, science, and reading that I can use in my newsletter."

Can you picture what kinds of images the chatbot might create in response? Try it out and see for yourself!

---

human hands and been dissatisfied with the results? They are notoriously difficult to represent correctly—perhaps because we are so familiar with our hands that we can immediately tell when there is something wrong in the rendering. I once read that the left hand of Leonardo da Vinci's *Mona Lisa* is held up by art historians as one of the most perfectly rendered hands ever, and it supposedly took the master Leonardo *years* to get that hand right. I don't know if that is a true story or not, but it always comes to mind for me when thinking about AI image generation.

AI Use Case

"I am a high school biology teacher, and I need an illustration for a worksheet I am creating that explains the structure of a virus. Generate an image of a phage virus that illustrates its protein coat and the way it can attach to the cell wall of a bacterium it is infecting. I won't need color images; shades of gray will work fine for this image."

Notice the content-specific wording in this prompt and the note about color not being necessary. You might try several different versions of this prompt and see what varieties you get in response.

"I am a middle school history teacher, and I use a storytelling approach to help history come to life for my students. We are currently learning about the history of ancient Rome, and I need a picture of Hannibal crossing the Alps with elephants that I can use a focusing image to capture their imaginations. Generate an image of Carthaginian soldiers and elephants coming down a mountainous pathway. Make them look like they are ready to fight: strong, well-armed, and led by a fearsome warrior-king."

When I tried this prompt, I was surprised how much it looked like a Renaissance-era painting. This had me wondering what other versions might be generated by tweaking the prompt: what if we would ask for a cartoon version? A photorealistic version? Remember that a more specific prompt might get you a result more closely aligned to exactly what you are imagining and that a few iterations might be needed.

I suspect you can already imagine ways students might also use image generation as part of their own creative work. There is potential for creating illustrations for all kinds of creative work! Consider a prompt like this: "I need a picture to illustrate a story I am writing about a polar bear who is riding an iceberg on a tour around Alaska. Generate a cartoon-like picture of a polar bear sitting on a floating chunk of ice, with snowy pine trees in the background." What kind of result might the student get? Coaching students in how to carefully craft a prompt to get an image that would be a useful illustration for their work is an important part of mentoring them into the appropriate, ethical use of AI.

I need to offer one more caveat for working with images: it is possible to upload an image and ask the AI to generate a modified version. While this can be useful in some situations—"Create a cartoon version of this image in the style of classic Hanna-Barbera animation"—I suspect you can imagine ways that this sort of prompting could go awry in a hurry. I would urge caution with this approach, of course! But it is worth exploring the potential of it; you might try it with an innocuous photo to see what kinds of results you might get.

GUIDANCE FOR USING THIS STRATEGY

I think there is a time and a place for using AI-generated images for student projects, but I would suggest it is not for every project. We should always be careful to not outsource our human creativity to the machines! Depending on the intended learning outcome, a student-created illustration in crayons, markers, or colored pencils might certainly be a better result, even if it is less "professional" than the computer-generated illustration.

The contours of the big story can certainly help us as we think about appropriate use of AI for generating images. First, when we think about Creation, generating images clearly aligns with the human impulse to create. We should keep clearly in mind that the way the AI generates is certainly different than human skill at creating with artistry, but this tool could definitely help us, particularly in specific situations where human artistry is not the goal. However, considering the Fall, there are also multiple places where the use of this tool could potentially go sideways: creating mean-spirited, hurtful images based on uploaded graphics is a very real possibility, as are God- and human-dishonoring prompts that would result in ugliness and potential to damage relationships. Discerning a redeemed and Restoration-oriented approach is key! The principles for ethical implementation may give helpful guidance for more redemptive and restorative uses of this capacity to generate images.

Illustrations are often part of a teachers' work, and the potential to generate graphics that are aligned to the specific needs and interests of your curriculum is one we should definitely consider! But, as always, discernment is required, and a focus on doing the right work is essential. If humans should be creating the work themselves, this could be a real opportunity for a "work is fun!" conversation with students.

KEY IDEA FROM THIS CHAPTER

AI tools can create graphics that can be used for a variety of situations. Careful, ethical usage is essential, and practice with the prompting will almost certainly help you get better results.

QUESTIONS FOR REFLECTION AND DISCUSSION

1. Considering the five principles for ethical implementation—privacy, relationships, integrity, transparency, and humility—what are some guidelines you will use to direct the use of AI to create images?

2. Try using the prompting suggestions in this chapter, but apply them to your own content, grade level, and context. What kind of results did you get? If you didn't get the results you were hoping for, what else could you try for prompting the chatbot?

29

AI Use Case
Personalized Tutoring Systems

THE BACKGROUND

The use cases for generative AI we've been considering so far have largely been focused on teachers' uses of these powerful tools. I'm generally much more comfortable with teachers being the ones using AI rather than the students. This is because an educator, as an adult with a pre-frontal cortex that is fully formed, ought to have better judgment about how to use AI with wisdom. (Note that I say, "ought to," because this certainly is not a given in this sin-stained world!) But I do think there are some potential uses for generative AI with students that we should consider.

In an earlier chapter, I mentioned how Carol Ann Tomlinson's work on differentiated instruction was transformative for my own teaching practice when I first encountered it in the early 2000s. I had always had a sense that lumping students together as "the class" and just teaching towards the middle wasn't working very well. But the thought of trying to individualize instruction for the many, many students who came through my middle school

AI Use Case

classroom every day felt far too overwhelming to even contemplate. Tomlinson's approach of providing different tiers of instruction to students with particular learner profiles, multiple pathways into the curriculum based on flexible grouping, or multiple possibilities for products students could create to demonstrate their learning clicked for me. As one teacher, I couldn't write sixty-five different lesson plans for the sixty-five grade-seven students who came through my classroom, but I could build in some flexibility for content, process, or product.

But what if we could leverage the power of generative AI to actually personalize learning for each of those sixty-five students? What could that look like? Is it feasible? And if it's feasible, is this something we should consider?

I think this is a really intriguing possibility, but one we should approach with caution. Particularly with a publicly available general purpose tool, like ChatGPT's free version, I am not sure this is a great idea. As a general caveat: according to ChatGPT's terms of service (and those of other generative AI tools) parental permission is required for kids ages 13–18, and children younger than 13 are not meant to use ChatGPT. So even if you could prompt the AI to function as a personalized tutor, this is probably not a great path forward. That said, there are some AI tools that are specifically designed for kids to be used in school settings, and those might be better options to consider. I want us to consider, however, how an AI chatbot might help fulfill the promise of personalized learning—but please consider these prompts to be an *example* to contemplate rather than a suggestion of "here's what you should do," okay? With that caution, have a look at how we might prompt the chatbot to function like a personalized tutor.

PROMPTING GENERATIVE AI

Reminder: this prompting example is an illustration for you to try so you can explore the possibility of this approach. It is *not* a recommendation for use with students.

Part VI: AI Use Cases

ChatGPT can function as a personalized tutor if you prompt it to behave in specific ways. Here are a few examples of things you might try:

"I want to learn more about music theory. I am a beginner, but I have a basic knowledge about how to read music. I want you to act as my personalized music theory tutor. I'm interested in learning music theory in a structured, step-by-step way. Please explain concepts clearly, give me specific examples I can try, and offer short practice exercises with feedback. Start with the most foundational topics, and help me build my understanding over time. I'd also like you to check my answers when I try exercises, explain any mistakes, and track my progress."

"I want you to act as my personal tutor to help me learn basic concepts in psychology. I know a few things about psychology already, but it's been a little while since I've studied it. I'm especially interested in how the brain works, how thinking and memory function, and major theories of cognitive development. Please explain things in a clear, beginner-friendly way, using specific examples when possible. Organize the material step-by-step, starting with foundational concepts in neuroscience and cognition. I'd also like occasional short quizzes or exercises to check my understanding, and I'd like you to track what I've learned so far and suggest what to study next. Let's begin with a basic overview of how the brain is structured and how it supports thinking and memory."

"I am a complete beginner and know virtually nothing about coding, but I want to learn the Python programming language. I want you to be my personalized tutor and teach me how to write good code in Python. Please explain everything in a straightforward, step-by-step way. Start with the absolute basics, like what programming is, how Python works, and how to write and run simple code. I'd like you to include examples, programming exercises I can try, and explanations of what each line of code does. Please check my answers when I try things, and correct me gently if I make mistakes. As I learn, help me build on what I've already learned and suggest what to study next."

Notice that in each of these prompts there is a suggestion for the level of understanding, as well as some specific things to include in the lessons. There are also ideas included in the prompts about how the instruction should unfold and how assessment and feedback should be incorporated. The idea here is that we are trying to tell the AI chatbot what we will need to be successful—leveraging what we know about what good instruction looks like and using our expertise as professional educators to tell it how to coach the learning in progress.

GUIDANCE FOR USING THIS STRATEGY

I am cautiously optimistic about the Restoration-oriented possibilities of personalized AI tutoring systems. After decades of trying to tailor my teaching to the needs of diverse students, this seems like an interesting possibility to make this more realistic without overwhelming the teacher.

That said, let's carefully consider how the big story might guide our use of personalized tutoring systems. If we view our students as uniquely created image-bearers, it follows that we should do our best to provide them uniquely tailored learning opportunities. Using the creational potential of the tools and resources we have that might help meet their learning needs seems a promising way to develop those kinds of tailored approaches. However, I wonder about whether this kind of tailoring might end up in *individualized* instruction rather than *personalized* instruction? As a result of the Fall, I think we are quick to jump to individualism in a way that minimizes the truth of how we are created to function in community. Does this kind of tutoring approach lead to more fracturing, splitting students apart rather than bringing them together? This requires some discernment, I think! Perhaps this is a case where there are multiple competing stories that we need to navigate with care and wisdom: students *are* unique individuals with their own gifts, talents, needs, strengths, and weaknesses, and they also function as a group, a microcosm of the body of Christ, where "the eye cannot say to the hand, 'I don't need you!' And the head cannot say to the feet, 'I don't need you!'"[1]

What do you think? Can a personalized approach to learning provided through an AI tutor be a Restoration-animated way of teaching?

KEY IDEA FROM THIS CHAPTER

Generative AI could be used to develop personalized tutoring systems, but free, publicly available AI chatbots are not a good pathway for doing this with students. Careful, ethical usage is essential, and tools designed for use by kids are a better option if teachers are planning to use or create AI tutors for their students.

QUESTIONS FOR REFLECTION AND DISCUSSION

1. Considering the five principles for ethical implementation—privacy, relationships, integrity, transparency, and humility—what are some guidelines you will use to inform the way you might use AI as a personalized tutor for your students?

2. Try using the prompting suggestions in this chapter, but apply them to your own content, grade level, and context. What kind of results did you get? If you didn't get the results you were hoping for, what else could you try for prompting the chatbot?

---

1. 1 Cor 12:21.

30

AI Use Case
Iterative Writing

THE BACKGROUND

Writing teachers often prompt students to complete multiple drafts of a work. In my experience, however, few students relish this work. Many seem to think that the first draft is "good enough," and the process of revision is wasted work. Perhaps some teachers even feel that way? That said, there *are* times when one draft is enough. But for beautiful work, a process of iteration and revision almost always results in a more elegant final product.

Perhaps this is an opportunity for teachers to help students practice and develop a "work is fun!" mindset? Let's consider that not every piece of work needs to be revised and polished. But for the ones that do, perhaps starting with "first draft, worst draft," and then iterating from there could be good path forward? I think part of the challenge for many teachers is the amount of sheer effort it takes to give students effective feedback on their writing—and the demand of wading through not-so-great writing on the path toward the final, beautiful result. Students can be trained to give good peer feedback, of course.[1] This also takes some intentional time and effort on the part of the teacher to provide this training. As you might suspect by now, I think it's important for teachers—and even fellow students—to practice this work of giving feedback to students on works-in-progress. But perhaps using an AI chatbot as part of the process of iteration could be a blessing for teachers who find themselves in this situation?

Similar to the example of personalized tutoring discussed in the last chapter, this approach is one for students interacting with the AI. The same caveat about the age of students is important to consider for ethical usage of the AI chatbot; according to the terms of service, most AI tools should not be used by students under the age of 13 and should have parental permission for ages 13–18, unless the tool is explicitly created for educational purposes. With that caveat in mind, consider how a chatbot might be used as part of an iterative writing process.

PROMPTING GENERATIVE AI

First off, you'll need a sample of writing to use this strategy. Write a short "first-draft, worst draft" piece that you can upload into the AI chatbot. Write a short piece of about one hundred words to have something to play around with. Maybe think of something you are going to be teaching soon, and write a description you could give to your students to explain the basic idea of the unit you are going to be teaching. For example, when I was a middle school science teacher, I taught a unit for seventh-graders that was a sort of introduction to living things, and I might have written this explanation:

> In our next unit, we are going to focus on a big question: What does it mean to be alive? We will try to define

---

1. One of my very favorite examples of students providing peer feedback is the story of "Austin's Butterfly," as recounted by master educator Ron Berger. If you have never seen it, you really should. It is about six minutes long, and it is six minutes well-spent for thinking about the important role that peer feedback can take, even with very young students. See EL Education, "Austin's Butterfly."

the differences between living and non-living things. An important term we will define and use throughout this unit will be the word "organism." An organism is a living thing. In this unit, we will learn the features that all organisms have in common, such as needing energy, needing raw materials, being able to reproduce, being able to grow and develop, having a life span, and more. We will explore the idea that living things are made of cells, and we will learn about the development of cell theory. We will focus on the idea that science develops over time, and as scientists learn more about the world, the mental models we use to explain the way the world works also progress—including our understanding of organisms."

I encourage you to write your own similar "first draft, worst draft" piece of writing to play with.

Okay, on to the prompting.

Once you have a short piece of writing ready for feedback, begin by prompting the chatbot with something like this:

> I am working on improving my writing skills. I will upload a piece of writing—please critique it, giving me feedback. Note areas that seem relatively strong, and explain why the writing is good. Likewise, note sections that could be improved, and coach me on what could be strengthened. Give me feedback on clarity, tone, structure, and grammar.

After this, upload your writing into the chatbot. See what kind of feedback you receive—you might be surprised!

As you are experimenting with this process, I encourage you to take all the chatbot's suggestions for improvements and make each change that was recommended.

Now, prompt the chatbot again. This time, try this prompt, or something like it: "I have revised my first draft to include your feedback. What is improved in this draft, and what should I still work on?"

Again, see what kind of feedback you receive, and decide whether to incorporate the feedback. And now, solicit more input from the chatbot, asking for suggestions for how to expand the work: "I have made further revisions, but now I need to expand my work. Give me some suggestions for related topics that I could write about."

Or perhaps: "This is the first paragraph of a longer work that I am going to be developing. In light of what I've written here, help me develop an outline for other topics that I could investigate."

Or even: "Given what I've written here, what else should I be thinking about related to this topic?"

You might be surprised by the results of these kinds of prompts!

If you are planning to use this kind of iterative writing process with students, I encourage to model this explicitly in front of them. Demonstrate exactly what you are doing: show them a "first draft, worst draft" writing example, and illustrate how you are prompting the AI for feedback—not asking the chatbot to do the writing but how to use it as a sort of writing coach to point out the strengths and areas for growth in the writing. After all, that's what we do as human writing coaches too: we don't do the writing for the students, but we support their own creativity and development. Let's foster this kind of "work is fun!" approach when it comes to writing and look for opportunities to create beautiful work.

GUIDANCE FOR USING THIS STRATEGY

Once again, let's consider how the shape of the big story can give us some guidance here. Our students, sinful as they are, might be tempted to use the AI to do the work for them. I fear that it is easy for students to short-circuit their own learning by just feeding a prompt into the AI chatbot and taking the result, so my hope in this strategy is to provide students with a model for honest, thoughtful work and learning. Modeling and encouraging are going to be key!

This strategy is a real opportunity for students to see the created goodness of hard work but also to see the ways that AI can help and support them in doing that hard work. Emphasizing that God created us to be creative—including through our writing— might be a helpful approach for you with your students.

AI Use Case

I think this is definitely a Restoration-oriented way to approach using AI with students. You might encourage students to submit each draft of their writing, along with the feedback they get from the AI chatbot, and also write a reflection on their process, including what they learned and how they felt about using the AI as a tool to support their creative work; this could be a real celebration of their work!

KEY IDEA FROM THIS CHAPTER

Generative AI can provide coaching for writing, noting both areas for improvement as well as sections that are well written. Deliberately teaching and modeling how to do this is essential for ensuring students use the AI in ethical ways to support their learning.

QUESTIONS FOR REFLECTION AND DISCUSSION

1. Considering the five principles for ethical implementation—privacy, relationships, integrity, transparency, and humility—what are some guidelines you will use to inform the way you might use AI to coach students through an iterative writing process?

2. Try using the prompting suggestions in this chapter, but apply them to your own content, grade level, and context. What kind of results did you get? If you didn't get the results you were hoping for, what else could you try for prompting the chatbot?

PART VII

A Theology of Educational Technology

31

Toward a Theology of Educational Technology

Living Faith in a Technology-Rich World

You might not think that the Bible mentions AI, but you would be mistaken. The Bible has very specific and unambiguous guidance about the right response to AI. Joshua 8:1a lays it out very clearly: "Then the Lord said to Joshua, 'Do not be afraid; do not be discouraged. Take the whole army with you, and go up and attack Ai.'"[1] It's pretty obvious what we are supposed to do here, right? God's word is clearly telling us that we need to go and smash those supercomputers, destroy the neural networks, and obliterate the large language models! Take the whole army with us, and let's get after it!

I hope you can infer from my tone that I am joking as I share this passage from Joshua with you. I do not think this is an appropriate use of Scripture at all; it is taken *wildly* out of context, of course! My pastor was recently teaching a sermon series on the book of Joshua, and when we were studying Josh 8, this verse caught my imagination—I was thinking a lot about writing this

---

1. Josh 8:1a.

Part VII: A Theology of Educational Technology

book at that time—I thought this was a cute example to illustrate how it is possible to misuse the Bible in our attempts to look for guidance and clear teaching from Scripture.

Please know that I hold a very high view of Scripture: I believe it is inspired by the Holy Spirit! But truly, I think there is a problem when we look to the Bible for specific, word-for-word teaching on every single topic in contemporary life. I am sure that there are people might be excited to hear this "clear teaching from Scripture"—that we should attack AI. That is not my argument here. My contention is that the Joshua example above is simply a *bad* reading of the Bible. This is the sort of problematic outcome that can result from trying to find a proof text from Scripture to support our argument or—more ominously—twisting Scripture out of context to try to make the Bible say something that it really isn't saying at all. If you read the rest of Josh 8 and put it in the broader context of the conquest of Canaan, you'll quickly see that this passage has *nothing* to do with our contemporary situation of trying to figure out how to live as faithful followers of Jesus in a world where AI exists.

In this section of this book, I want to encourage us to develop a sort of "theology of educational technology." What I mean by this is that there are many topics in life that the Bible obviously teaches us about, but there are others that are less clear or not addressed at all. For example, the word "computer" does not appear in Scripture. But does that mean the Bible has nothing to say about how we should think about technology? I think there are plenty of biblical principles we can and should draw upon as we consider the right place of computer technology in our lives, even though the Bible was written long before the digital age. This sort of theological thinking is what I'm aiming towards.

My friend Derek Schuurman is a committed Christ-follower who serves as a professor of computer science. I appreciate his take on this idea of applying biblical principles to the way we consider technology. To help us begin to consider a theological approach toward technology, Schuurman riffs on the church father Tertullian, who famously asked, "What does Athens have to do with

Toward a Theology of Educational Technology

Jerusalem?" This question is meant to evoke a real wondering for Christians and how we make our way through this world. Tertullian is asking us to consider what culture (represented by Athens) has to do with faith (represented by Jerusalem). Schuurman reframes this by asking, "'What does Silicon Valley have to do with Jerusalem?' or to put it another way, 'What do bytes have to do with beliefs?'"[2] What Dr. Schuurman is really getting at, in my estimation, could also be framed as "what does it mean to have a living faith in a technology-rich world?" Or, perhaps more specifically for us as educators, maybe the question is "how should a Christian educator use technology for teaching and learning?" Or, even more specifically, "how does AI connect with teaching Christianly?"

Because the Bible doesn't *directly* address this question, we need do a little careful exploration of Scripture to make application to our particular time and place. The very real challenge for those of us who want to use the Bible as guidance for how we ought to live: not every topic under the sun is directly addressed in God's word. So, let's get ready to think theologically—not slavishly searching for proof texts but discerning big-picture principles that can guide us into wisdom.

KEY IDEA FROM THIS CHAPTER

The Bible is the inspired word of God, but it does not specifically address every topic under the sun; learning to think theologically and use biblical principles can help us respond to the issues of the day with wisdom.

---

2. This quote comes from p. 4 of Schuurman's wonderful, thought-provoking article "Technology and the Biblical Story," which begins with these questions.

Part VII: A Theology of Educational Technology

QUESTIONS FOR REFLECTION AND DISCUSSION

1. What was your reaction to the Josh 8:1a passage? What might that reaction reveal about the way you think about Scripture?

2. What comes to mind for you when you think of a "theology of educational technology"? What kinds of biblical principles might there be that can guide us to using technology wisely for teaching and learning?

32

Education as Formation
More Than Information Transfer

WHAT DOES IT MEAN to become educated?

Some people might consider education as amassing knowledge. There are things I did not know, but now I have learned them and I know them, so I am educated. I am fully acquainted with a topic, and I can repeat back the essential facts to you to demonstrate my knowledge. How does that sound? Would you consider that "enough" to be educated?

Knowledge is necessary for education, surely. But is it enough? Perhaps we might go deeper than knowledge, to understanding. To understand something is more than just knowing about it—understanding suggests a deep familiarity that is more robust than the basic facts. Understanding suggests a framework for putting the facts together and perhaps even the ability to apply knowledge to novel situations. Is understanding "enough" to be considered educated?

Understanding and the application of knowledge are definitely aspects of becoming educated, but I want to urge us to consider a deeper aspect to education. I believe that education is really aimed at much more than information. If you are truly educated, you should *be different* than you were before. Education should *do something* to you. It's more than just knowing or even understanding. To become educated means becoming something more than you were before.

In other words, I believe that education—a real and true education—is much more than mastering *information*. Education is a matter of *formation*. And the things we do as we are learning—becoming educated—are the habits that will lead to *transformation*.[1] Christian philosopher James K. A. Smith encourages us to ask the question "Do you ever experience a gap between what you *know* and what you *do*? Have you ever found that new knowledge and information don't seem to translate into a new way of life? . . . What if it's because you aren't just a thinking thing?"[2] This idea might be challenging for us as educators, because we often emphasize the cognitive aspects of learning—amassing knowledge and developing understanding. It's important, then, for us to remember a bigger story of who we are and how we are created to be.

Remember Andy Crouch's definition of what it means to be human? Using Jesus' teaching about the greatest commandment in Mark 12, Crouch encourages us to consider that "every human person is a heart-soul-mind-strength complex designed for love."[3] If we reduce our humanness to thinking *only* about the "mind" part, we are neglecting important parts of what it truly means to be human!

I think there is a real challenge for us as educators, and as users of digital technologies, to reduce human beings to their minds. This is not something that has just come up in the age of AI. The initial promise of the Internet was that all the information humans had amassed would be freely and easily available. What an asset for educators! All that knowledge, ripe for the picking!

---

1. This is the whole premise of Smith's book *You Are What You Love*. It's a wonderful book about the "spiritual power of habit"—and how the things we practice eventually become habits, and the habits we exhibit demonstrate what we truly love.
2. Smith, *You Are What You Love*, 5.
3. Crouch, *Life We're Looking For*, 33.

Education as Formation

It would be silly to say that the Internet did not impact education, of course. But did free access to information *transform* education? I'm not so sure about that.

Having more knowledge available to us might seem on the surface to make us more educated, but I don't believe this is necessarily the case. It's not as though I have just downloaded Wikipedia into my brain so I have all the facts at my immediate disposal. And, speaking of Wikipedia—and the Internet in general—how do I know what I'm reading is factual, accurate, and true?

This is my argument for education being more than information transfer. We need a context to make sense of the information, to make it meaningful, to make a difference for my life.

What I'm actually arguing for here is more than knowledge. We need *wisdom*. And wisdom takes formation.

Thinking theologically, my mind immediately jumps to Proverbs: "The fear of the Lord is the beginning of knowledge, but fools despise wisdom and instruction."[4] Our knowledge of God is the *beginning of knowledge*. The teacher in Proverbs describes the path of wisdom: "I instruct you in the way of wisdom and lead you along straight paths. When you walk, your steps will not be hampered; when you run, you will not stumble."[5] And how do we come to know this path? Psalm 119 is instructive: "Your word is a lamp for my feet, a light on my path."[6] God's word is instructive for the path we should follow, the path of wisdom. The apostle Paul echoes this in his instruction to Timothy: "All Scripture is God-breathed and is useful for teaching, rebuking, correcting and training in righteousness, so that the servant of God may be thoroughly equipped for every good work."[7] And here we come to that point about formation: Scripture points us towards wisdom and provides us with guidance for the equipping for "every good work"—which I take to mean there is a way of *living* that is more than just "knowing." This is what I mean by education as

4. Prov 1:7.
5. Prov 4:11–12.
6. Ps 119:105.
7. 2 Tim 3:16–17.

Part VII: A Theology of Educational Technology

formation: it is doing something to us, changing us, transforming us into something more than we were before.

My friend Syd Hielema is a theologian and biblical scholar. Years ago, we were talking about the opportunities Christian educators have to speak into the lives of the students they serve, and he said, "Faith formation is sort of like trying to nail Jell-O to the wall. It's hard to pin down! And wisdom is more often *caught* than *taught*." That idea has always stuck with me. Hielema is drawing on biblical wisdom in this teaching as well; I think he is right in line with Moses' encouragement to the people of Israel as he began to teach them God's law: "These commandments that I give you today are to be on your hearts. Impress them on your children. Talk about them when you sit at home and when you walk along the road, when you lie down and when you get up. Tie them as symbols on your hands and bind them on your foreheads. Write them on the doorframes of your houses and on your gates."[8] It's not that we can't teach through explicit instruction. But wisdom forms through relationships, and those relationships are where real transformation takes place—a true education! This kind of education is more than just for our minds; being in relationship this way is a "heart-soul-mind-strength designed for love" kind of opportunity for formation.

To bring this back around to our conversation about technology and education, let's consider a few questions:

- If it's true that education is more than information, how will our teaching practices emphasize the holistic nature of what it means to be human?
- If it's true that education is more than information, how will the tools we choose be part of developing wisdom and not just defaulting to information transfer?
- If it's true that education is more than information, how will technologies we utilize for teaching and learning help us grow as faithful followers of Jesus—and help us disciple our students?

8. Deut 6:6–9.

Education as Formation

- If it's true that education is more than information, how does our imagination, informed by the big story of Scripture, give us a better story to invite students into?

As we consider the pressures that an AI-infused educational environment can bring, let's strive to become educators who won't settle for an information transfer sort of "education." Let's commit to a robust, fully formed education as formation!

KEY IDEA FROM THIS CHAPTER

Education is a matter of formation—becoming wise people who live and act differently—rather than simple transfer of information.

QUESTIONS FOR REFLECTION AND DISCUSSION

1. Evaluate your own teaching practice: where are you settling for education as information transfer? Where are you striving for education as formation?
2. Revisit those four questions at the end of this chapter: how would you answer those questions, and how might they inform how you will move forward with regard to generative AI?

33

The Role of Doubt
Cultivating a Humble Skepticism

NEIL POSTMAN WAS A prophet. I don't mean that he spoke for God in a biblical sense; I actually don't know what Postman's religious beliefs were. But as a professor of communication studies at New York University for decades, Postman was an astute cultural critic, and he spoke out carefully and thoughtfully about where he saw things going wrong, culturally speaking. His book *Technopoly* was published in 1992, before the rise of the World Wide Web, but in it, he was able to accurately predict where American culture would land thirty years down the road.[1]

In chapter 4 of *Technopoly*, Postman recounts an experiment he used to do with friends to illustrate the challenges of information overload. He would ask a colleague, "Did you read the newspaper today?" If the answer was "yes," that was the end of the experiment. But if the unsuspecting target said "no," Postman would

---

1. I first read *Technopoly* when I was taking a course on educational technology for my master's degree in the early 2000s. I honestly did not appreciate the book very much when I first read it, but in the intervening years I've reread it several times, and I've come to see his cultural analysis as unsettlingly accurate. I believe it's an important book for us to consider as we think about the right place of technology in our lives.

The Role of Doubt

continue, making an outlandish claim—completely made-up, of course—along the lines of "well, there was a story about a scientific study that showed that eating a diet of only chocolate eclairs can lead to serious weight loss. There is some chemical in the eclairs that causes people to quickly drop pounds." And Postman's report was that about two-thirds of his targets would say something like, "Huh... I think I've heard something about that." Postman's point: we are quick to believe—or at least, not *disbelieve*—even the most ridiculous claims.[2]

Friends, take note that Postman was doing this experiment in the early 1990s, before the Internet was mainstream, before social media's ubiquity, before the echo-chambers of personalized feeds driven by algorithms. Postman describes this as a problem of information glut, and he suggests that technology is a substantial part of the problem, generating more and more data which leads to an overwhelming flood of information. He suggests, "When the supply of information is no longer controllable, a general breakdown in psychic tranquility and social purpose occurs. Without defenses, people have no way of finding meaning in their experiences, lose their capacity to remember, and have difficulty imagining reasonable futures."[3] I agree with Postman in this, and I think that this situation is far more problematic in our contemporary moment. My take: we need to embrace a humble sort of skepticism. We should practice doubt, but we should do this with kindness and gentleness—loving our neighbors as we love ourselves.

For example, we might hear extraordinary claims about new technologies—like generative AI, perhaps?—along the lines of "this will revolutionize teaching and learning!" or "if you don't get on board with embracing this technology, your students will be left behind!" or "this is going to be the end of education as we know it, and we have to ban it!" Each of these claims is extraordinary, and the person making the declaration almost certainly has a reason

---

2. Postman, *Technopoly*, 56–57. He goes on to explain much of his concern—even in the early 1990s—that people were far too quick to trust without asking questions to verify extraordinary claims.

3. Postman, *Technopoly*, 72.

Part VII: A Theology of Educational Technology

for making that passionate statement. But can we discern what is behind these kinds of claims?

I will admit that I'm a technophile—I love technology, and I gravitate towards novelty and innovation. But I'm also skeptical of the claims of technology companies who are promising panaceas that will magically solve all our problems with the latest tech tools/toys. I want us to learn to distinguish sharply, to think critically, and to judge wisely. I don't think we should immediately, wholeheartedly embrace new technologies. But neither do I think we should immediately ban new innovations. We must cultivate a sort of healthy skepticism of technology—in ourselves and in our students as well.

Carrying forward the development of a theology of educational technology, let's consider what this kind of careful discernment could look like. We are living in a particular cultural context, one Postman names a "technopoly." How shall we respond with wisdom? In Rom 12:2, Paul encourages the Roman Christians—and us too—"do not conform to the pattern of this world, but be transformed by the renewing of your mind. Then you will be able to test and approve what God's will is—his good, pleasing and perfect will." John encourages us to likewise "test the spirits" of our age,[4] and I think that a cultural love of technology—and technicism—is certainly a spirit of the age that we need to discern. This is the sort of healthy skepticism I'm suggesting: we need to rely on the wisdom of the Spirit so that we can discern the spirits.[5]

Jesus himself encourages wise discernment in his disciples, but take note of *how* Jesus encourages them—and us—to do this. When he sends his disciples out on their first adventure in preaching about the kingdom of God, he admonishes them, "I am sending you out as sheep in the midst of wolves, so be wise

---

4. See 1 John 4, for this encouragement, which includes this wisdom: "Dear friends, do not believe every spirit, but test the spirits to see whether they are from God" (1 John 4:1a).

5. See 1 Cor 2:6–16 for some of Paul's teaching on how the Spirit imparts wisdom to believers.

as serpents and innocent as doves."[6] We might not immediately link wisdom and innocence this way, but it certainly is the way of the kingdom! My suggestion for us in thinking about how we can express our skepticism is to do so humbly, along the lines of what Peter admonishes, to "do this with gentleness and respect, keeping a clear conscience."[7] We need to embody the fruit of the Spirit in all aspects of our lives, but this certainly includes the way we might express doubts in the face of bold claims. What good is it to be "right" if we are not also loving, kind, and good?[8] Fundamentally, I believe that a humble skepticism looks like expressing doubt in a way that demonstrates that we are seeking to live as disciples of Jesus.

When it comes to determining which technologies we should embrace and which we should exclude, wisdom is necessary. As we consider the way we discern the right place of technology in our classrooms—and in our lives—perhaps a wise series of questions to ask would include:

- What does this technology promise?
- How likely is it to fulfill that promise?
- If I use this technology, what will I gain and what will I lose?
- Can I use this technology in ways that work towards love, joy, peace, patience, kindness, goodness, faithfulness, gentleness, and self-control?

As we consider generative AI in particular, discernment is needed! We certainly need to be wise as serpents and innocent as doves—practicing humble skepticism.

---

6. Matt 10:16 (ESV).

7. 1 Pet 3:15b–16a. In this passage, Peter is encouraging the church to always be ready to answer people who ask us about the reason for our hope. But recognizing that others might misinterpret our peculiar way of being in the world, Peter admonishes us to gentleness.

8. Consider this list as the best way of being Jesus' people: "But the fruit of the Spirit is love, joy, peace, patience, kindness, goodness, faithfulness, gentleness, and self-control" (Gal 5:22–23a ESV).

Part VII: A Theology of Educational Technology

KEY IDEA FROM THIS CHAPTER

Developing wisdom for how we use technology means increasing our capacity for discernment and living it out with the fruit of the Spirit.

QUESTIONS FOR REFLECTION AND DISCUSSION

1. Imagine you were confronted with an extremely unlikely claim, like Postman's chocolate eclairs experiment. What would a "humble skepticism" response look like? What kind of script could you create to answer an extraordinary assertion like this?

2. Revisit those four questions at the end of this chapter: how would you answer those questions, and how might they inform how you will move forward with regard to generative AI?

34

The Arc of the Redemptive Story
From the Garden to the City

THROUGHOUT THIS BOOK, I'VE been encouraging us to develop a Christian imagination for AI specifically and technology more generally. The big story of Scripture is a key part of understanding what this imagination looks like.

When we consider Creation, we are thinking about how things are supposed to be—how God created all things and described them as "good"—even "very good."

When we consider the Fall, we are intentionally naming the ways that sin has twisted and tarnished everything. While we can still discern the goodness of Creation, the pollution of sin is everywhere.

When we consider Redemption, we are celebrating Jesus' salvage operation. He has saved us from the debt of our sin, and he has bought back all things. The brokenness of sin is fully addressed, and Christ is sovereign over all things because his death and resurrection has won the day!

When we consider Restoration, we are looking forward to the time when God will make all things new. In the meantime, we find that while God certainly does not *need* us (he is the all-powerful, all-knowing, completely self-sufficient God, after all!), he loves us and invites us to participate in working towards Restoration, which he will complete when Jesus returns.

This arc of the big story helps us remember who we are and whose we are. But I think it also reveals something important for us about the right role of technology in our lives.

Notice that there is a progression happening, an unfolding that develops throughout the big story. We begin the story in the garden.[1] But the end of the story is not a return to Eden; we end up in a city, the new Jerusalem.[2] We begin in the garden, but we don't end up there. The big story illustrates a sort of technological progression, moving from the garden to the city! I take great comfort in this fact. This means that technological development is not separate from God's plan or outside of his sovereignty.

There are a variety of word-pictures throughout Scripture that help us imagine what the restored Creation—including examples of technology—will look like at the Restoration of all things. The prophet Micah uses the imagery of turning swords and spears into plowshares and pruning hooks,[3] reworking technologies designed to damage and destroy into tools of cultivation. The prophet Zechariah describes the Restoration to come on the day of the Lord as being marked by even mundane technologies like

---

1. See Gen 2 for the beginning of the story, in Eden. Notably, "The Lord God took the man and put him in the Garden of Eden to work it and take care of it" (Gen 2:15). The human story within Act I of the big story (Creation) certainly begins in the garden.

2. See Rev 21 for the end of the story, in the new Jerusalem. Again, we should note, "I saw the Holy City, the new Jerusalem, coming down out of heaven from God, prepared as a bride beautifully dressed for her husband. And I heard a loud voice from the throne saying, 'Look! God's dwelling place is now among the people, and he will dwell with them. They will be his people, and God himself will be with them and be their God'" (Rev 21:2–3). The story in Act IV of the big story (Restoration) ends up in the city!

3. Micah 4:3 says, "He will judge between many peoples and will settle disputes for strong nations far and wide. They will beat their swords into plowshares and their spears into pruning hooks. Nation will not take up sword against nation, nor will they train for war anymore."

The Arc of the Redemptive Story

bells on horses and cooking pots being made holy.[4] And we should remember that at the end of the big story in Rev 21, John hears Jesus himself declaring, "I am making everything new!"[5]

Paul teaches us that Jesus' redeeming work was to reconcile *all things* to God—and this means *all things* are included the Restoration to come.[6] That's a good reminder for us about what the Restoration really means: it's *not* that God is making "new things." Rather, he is making all things *new*.[7] The action of Restoration is the culmination of the love story that the big story of Scripture truly is: God loves his Creation, and though it is broken in the Fall, he Redeems it, and ultimately God will Restore all things to the way they are supposed to be.

We can find technology throughout the contours of the big story, and there is good news for us in this as we consider things like the right place of AI in education. Technology is part of the created order of things. Technology, like all things, is impacted by the Fall, which means it can be used in ways that are counter to the kingdom of God. But Christ's Redemption extends to all things, meaning that even those sinful uses of technology can be redirected—technology is under Christ's sovereign rule. And when Christ comes again, technology too will find its full restoration.

While we are living in these in-between times, looking forward to the new Jerusalem, we can work to use technology in Restoration-oriented ways. What might this look like? Here a few questions that might guide our use of technology towards Restoration:

---

4. Zechariah 14:20 says, "On that day holy to the Lord will be inscribed on the bells of the horses, and the cooking pots in the Lord's house will be like the sacred bowls in front of the altar."

5. Rev 21:5.

6. In Col 1, Paul describes the supremacy of Christ and includes this comment: "God was pleased to have all his fullness dwell in him [that is, Jesus], and through him to reconcile to himself all things, whether things on earth or things in heaven, by making peace through his blood, shed on the cross" (Col 1:19–20).

7. Derek Schuurman includes this idea on p. 9 of his article "Technology and the Biblical Story."

Part VII: A Theology of Educational Technology

- How could this technology, used rightly, bring glory to God?
- How could this technology, used rightly, emphasize the heart-soul-mind-strength nature of what it means to be human?
- How could this technology, used rightly, help us to be more loving to our neighbors and ourselves?
- What would using this technology look like if it were in the new Jerusalem?

That last question in particular might be a strange one for us to picture in reality. Will AI be part of the restored Creation? I truly don't know, but I like to imagine the possibility!

KEY IDEA FROM THIS CHAPTER

The big story of Scripture points us in a direction and shows us the unfolding of the kingdom of God in a way that can help us imagine the role of technological development.

QUESTIONS FOR REFLECTION AND DISCUSSION

1. Can you imagine technology in the new Jerusalem? What could a computer, a smartphone, or generative AI look like in the restored Creation?
2. Revisit those four questions at the end of this chapter: how would you answer those questions, and how might they inform how you will move forward with regard to generative AI?

PART VIII

Launching into the Future

35

Christian Education and AI
Where Are We Headed?

WE BEGAN THE JOURNEY of this book with a story from thirty years ago, with my first adventure on the World Wide Web. I shared how in those early years of my teaching career, my colleagues and I were confronted with the pressures of incorporating the Internet into our teaching, and as we considered the possibilities and pitfalls of this endeavor, there were a few basic postures that emerged:

- Some argued for a full embrace of this new technology, as it had the potential to transform education as we know it—and the students were going to use it anyway.
- Some argued that we had to ban it, because it had the potential to fundamentally damage students' learning.
- Some wondered just how worried we should be and would have preferred to simply ignore it.

The truth is, I think, somewhere inside the triangle formed by these positions. The Internet certainly impacted education—in some positive ways, in some negative ways—and we certainly can't ignore the Internet as an influence in education. Honestly, I can hardly imagine teaching without Internet access today, even though I could not have predicted back in 1995 just how much of an impact it would have had on the world of teaching and learning by 2025.

I wonder if we might wind up saying something similar thirty years on from today about the influence of AI on education. How will the world of teaching and learning shift by 2055 because of the influence of generative AI?

I think those same postures are present in the conversation today:

- Some folks are ready to throw the doors wide open and fully incorporate AI into education, whether out of pragmatism or optimism.
- Some folks are primed to (try to) ban access to generative AI, as all they see are the downsides.
- Some folks are wishing to just hide their heads in the sand and try to ignore it all.

By now, I hope that you, like me, are in a discerning space, recognizing that none of these three postures is adequate for responding to both the potential opportunities and possible risks that AI brings with it into our schools. I wish there was a tidy formula we could apply to help us navigate these uncharted waters, but I have not yet found it.

That said, think back over where we've been in this book. We've considered the fact that we all have some sort of imagination already for what AI is and what it is capable of—and we thought through the cultural influences that have shaped that imagination. We've explored the big story of Scripture as a better influence on our imaginations—the realest, truest story of them all—and considered what it means to be a human being in light of that big story. We've investigated how AI actually works in an attempt to demystify it a bit and better understand the possibilities and constraints of large language models. We've intentionally contemplated the work of teaching and learning, considering what AI might be able to do for us, and some concerns we should avoid. We imagined some possible use cases for AI in education and tried to align them to the contours of the big story, as well as a framework for ethical usage of AI. And finally, we pondered what a theology of educational technology might look like to carefully measure the ways we allow powerful technologies—including generative AI—to find a place in our lives. Does this give us "the answer"?

I am not sure we have a firm, clear, obvious answer. But I am bold enough to say that I am going to keep on exploring how I will use generative AI in my own life and in my teaching practice. I am going to move forward cautiously, and I'm going to seek to work with wisdom and discernment. But I am not going to be proceed in fear. I find myself somewhere in the midst of that triangle of excitement, uncertainty, and apprehension when it comes to generative AI, but I'm not landing in any of those corners.

Friends, we have the opportunity to imagine a future—with all the joys and concerns that might come—and we can do so in confidence, because God is in control. In fact, there is not a square inch in the whole domain of our human existence over which Christ, who is sovereign over all, does not cry "mine!"[1] This is good news, friends! As Christ's disciples, we can explore and discern where AI fits in the endeavor of teaching and learning with a humble boldness as we seek to serve the King and work to build his kingdom.

Grace and peace to you all as you seek to faithfully follow Jesus in your teaching and in your learning.

KEY IDEA FROM THIS CHAPTER

We are still at the beginning of the adventures to come with AI in education, and the good news is that God is sovereign over all things!

---

1. This is a commonly quoted passage from a speech by the Dutch theologian, Abraham Kuyper. Kuyper's actual original version used "thumb-breadth" instead of "square inch"—and the speech was given in Dutch, so this is a translation. See Roger Henderson's article, "Kuyper's Inch" for more on both the history of this phrase, as well as its implications for the Christian life.

Part VIII: Launching into the Future

QUESTIONS FOR REFLECTION AND DISCUSSION

1. What difference does it make for you to recognize that all things—including AI—are subject to Christ's rule and reign?

2. As we conclude our reading of this book, evaluate your thinking now about the role of AI in education. Has your thinking changed as you have read and reflected? Why or why not?

Bibliography

Bailey, Justin Ariel. *Interpreting Your World: Five Lenses for Engaging Theology and Culture*. Grand Rapids: Baker, 2022.
Campbell, Joseph. *The Hero with a Thousand Faces*. 2nd ed. Princeton, NJ: Princeton University Press, 1949.
Crouch, Andy. *The Life We're Looking For: Reclaiming Relationship in a Technological World*. New York: Convergent, 2022.
EL Education. "Austin's Butterfly: Models, Critique, and Descriptive Feedback." Oct. 4, 2016. YouTube video, 6:32. https://www.youtube.com/watch?v=E_6PskE3zfQ.
Henderson, Roger. "Kuyper's Inch." *Pro Rege* 36 (2008) 12–14.
Khan, Salman. *Brave New Words: How AI Will Revolutionize Education (And Why That's a Good Thing)*. New York: Viking, 2024.
Lang, James M. *Small Teaching: Everyday Lessons from the Science of Learning*. Hoboken, NJ: John Wiley & Sons, 2021.
Lewis, C. S. *The Lion, the Witch, and the Wardrobe*. Deluxe ed. New York: Harper Collins, 1997.
Losh, Elizabeth. *The War on Learning: Gaining Ground in the Digital University*. Cambridge, MA: MIT Press, 2014.
MacKenzie, Gordon. *Orbiting the Giant Hairball: A Corporate Fool's Guide to Surviving with Grace*. New York: Viking, 1996.
Magic School. "Terms of Service." Aug. 2024. https://www.magicschool.ai/privacy-security/terms-of-service.
Mulder, David J. *Always Becoming, Never Arriving: Developing an Imagination for Teaching Christianly*. Eugene, OR: Cascade, 2024.
Postman, Neil. *Technopoly: The Surrender of Culture to Technology*. New York: Vintage, 1992.
Rowling, J. K. *Harry Potter and the Deathly Hallows*. New York: Arthur A. Levine, 2007.
Schuurman, Derek. "Technology and the Biblical Story." *Pro Rege* 46 (2014) 4–11.
Smith, James K. A. *You Are What You Love: The Spiritual Power of Habit*. Grand Rapids: Brazos, 2016.

Bibliography

―――. *Desiring the Kingdom: Worship, Worldview, and Cultural Formation.* Grand Rapids: Baker, 2009.

Tangerman, Victor. "Sam Altman Admits That OpenAI Doesn't Actually Understand How Its AI Works." *Futurism*, Jun. 2024. https://futurism.com/sam-altman-admits-openai-understand-ai.

Tomlinson, Carol Ann. *Fulfilling the Promise of the Differentiated Classroom: Strategies and Tools for Responsive Teaching.* Alexandria, VA: ASCD, 2003.

Turing, Alan Mathison. "Computing Machinery and Intelligence." *Mind* 49 (1950) 433–60.

Turkle, Sherry. *Alone Together: Why We Expect More from Technology and Less from Each Other.* New York: Basic, 2011.

Van Dyk, John. *The Craft of Christian Teaching: A Classroom Journey.* Sioux Center, IA: Dordt, 2001.

Wolters, Albert M. *Creation Regained: Biblical Basics for a Reformational Worldview.* Grand Rapids: Eerdmans, 2005.

www.ingramcontent.com/pod-product-compliance
Lightning Source LLC
Chambersburg PA
CBHW071230170426
43191CB00032B/1307